POLYESTER
PEOPLE

RON VIETTI

POLYESTER PEOPLE
Copyright © 2010 by Ron Vietti

ISBN: 978-0-9845874-0-7

Published by

LIFEBRIDGE
BOOKS
P.O. BOX 49428
CHARLOTTE, NC 28277

Printed in the United States of America.

CONTENTS

PREFACE

Polyester suits were really cool in the 1970s, but the '70s are over.

Let's face it. Those polyester suits were never really natural to begin with. They were made from a combination of chemicals and were known for their ability to always look good without any noticeable wrinkles.

Even though they came from inexpensive, compound materials, they made the wearer look better. Now they may have gotten the job done in the '70s, but they are a real fashion no-no in this century; however, that doesn't stop a lot of people (who may be stuck in the '70s) from wearing them today. It's a cheap way to dress compared to buying the real thing made of wool or a combination of other fabrics.

In today's Christian world, many of our brothers and sisters are still opting out for the imitation Christian lifestyle that I often refer to as AC—American Christianity, which is comprised of little to no real substance. It's a cheap way to go, but just as polyester had its day, its time is over. This Christian lifestyle consisting of little to no prayer, limited knowledge of God's Word, and a severe lack of radical works will not cut it anymore.

We live in a society that is burned out on things that are not real in the church world. Just as people who wear polyester have no clue about how silly they look to a fashion-conscious culture, the hypocritical believer doesn't realize just how much he's hurting the cause of Christ. While thinking he is cool, the polyester believer has no clue that the world is laughing behind his back. What he thinks is spiritual, unbelievers view as silly and mundane.

For example, the world can't relate to long, boring church services and conversations inundated with phrases such as "Hallelujah," "Praise the Lord," and "Thank ya, Jesus."

We say that God is alive, but the world never sees Him active in our lives. Until we show them something real, they will keep on laughing at us.

Maybe you didn't know, but polyester melts at medium to high temperatures. As society continues to deteriorate, I'm afraid that it's just a matter of time before our plastic façade will begin to melt away, and we will be left standing naked for all to see. Then maybe we will turn to God, and He will replace our polyester suits with an old fashioned pair of blue jeans and a sports shirt—and then the world will begin to relate to us.

You don't have to look different to be different. In the church today, we put so much effort into changing the outside but put so little effort into changing the inside. We have grown so accustomed to what we think a Christian should look like that when we are exposed to the New Testament model of Christianity, we don't even recognize it. It is about the God who wants to live His life through us.

In this book, I hope I can show you how to draw closer to God than you've ever been before. Let's remove the polyester suits from the closet and be done with them once and for all and become the people God wants us to be. Then we will be able to relate to the 21st century world.

INTRODUCTION

The American church is full of people that we quickly identify as believers. But the question that begs to be answered today is believers in what? Do we believe in prayer? I doubt it when the average time a believer spends in prayer is less than three minutes a day. We profess to believe in the Holy Spirit, but how many times do we call upon Him in any given day? We boast in being people who live by the values of the Holy Bible, but the majority of Christians can't even recite the Ten Commandments or tell you where they are found in scripture, much less tell you the names of the twelve apostles. Something is dreadfully wrong within the ranks of Christendom.

The only angels we know anything about are the ones that hang on our Christmas trees during the holiday season or are portrayed on the decorated Christmas cards we send out every year. We don't dare acknowledge that we actually believe in demon spirits for fear that our peers would quickly write us off as more than a little wacky.

We want very little to do with Christian people who boast that they actually have a personal relationship with God—those who believe that God breaks through all the confusion and noise this world inundates us with and speaks to us as a father would with his own child. All of this kind of stuff is reserved for fanatics, the kind of individuals we have been taught to avoid at all costs; yet we fail to see that such people founded our faith. Men and women who saw nothing wrong with asking God to make His will known by drawing lots, people who spoke to demons like they would to a wayward dog that came uninvited into their yard to create havoc. These individuals, who gave definition to what it was to be a believer, didn't have to think twice about bringing up the subject of angels in a biblical discourse concerning everyday life.

The lifestyle of the New Testament Christian and the lifestyle of the average American Christian are worlds apart, and the chasm is growing wider every year. What can we do in order to regain our New Testament Christian roots and once again live with a spirit of awe?

It's pertinent today that all believers find their purpose in this world and fulfill their mission in life. It is essential that we spend time getting to know the God of the Bible. There are so many believing men and women who are getting highly involved in the kingdom; however, they have no clue as to who God really is, nor do they know how He wants to work through their lives.

There are so many varied opinions of God in the church world that it's plumb scary. To some, God doesn't speak to His children; to others, God never stops talking.

Will the way we see God communicating with His kids affect the outcome of our mission in life? Some people believe God heals the sick and always responds to praying over the hurting. But others see Him as unable or unwilling to respond to such prayers. Again, depending upon which way you believe, will it have an effect on your mission? Do you believe God speaks to His children in a way that can be understood? Does He still heal today? Does He still deliver today? Does He answer all of your prayers, some of your prayers, or none of them? Will God send angels to your rescue when you're in dire need? Or is God far removed from what goes on in your daily life?

What you believe in these areas will not have mere minor

effects on the outcome of your mission, but will have *drastic* effects.

In this book, I hope to push you into a new quest for answers to questions that, quite possibly, you've never been interested in asking before. I pray you will gain a new spiritual thirst for more of the biblical God than you've ever previously experienced. So lay all preconceived ideas aside that you've been taught in the American church and prepare to reexamine some biblical truths I believe will dramatically change your life.

One

RECAPTURING THE REAL DEAL

*I can tell you that God is alive
because I talked to Him this morning.*

— BILLY GRAHAM

As I was preparing a study in the New Testament one day, it suddenly dawned on me that the New Testament church and the American church have very little in common. Our values, our lifestyles, and the way we spend our time are totally different. Our belief system is based upon, pretty much, totally opposite things. It would probably be very difficult to convince an uninformed bystander that we were one in the same entity. For example, the early church in the book of Acts believed in spirits and dealt with them on somewhat of a regular basis. They openly spoke of the deeds of the Holy Spirit and lived in a spirit of awe.

Almost weekly, I get so excited about sharing from the pulpit something that has happened in my life or in the life of someone around me. I hope to accomplish two things by doing this. First, I want to show people that not only do I preach about a loving, living God who wants to interact in our daily lives, but I also experience the things I preach about. After all, if it doesn't work in my own life, maybe I shouldn't be preaching about it from the pulpit. But it does work—and that's the exciting part.

Second, I want to encourage people to imitate my lifestyle as I imitate Christ's. I want them to experience the same spirit of awe as I do on nearly a weekly basis.

STOP LOSING SLEEP

Let me give you an example of a couple of things that God has done in my life recently. A couple of years ago, I returned home about 2 A.M. from our church in Las Vegas, Nevada. I couldn't sleep because of some things that were on my mind, so I stayed awake all night praying and talking to God. To be quite honest, I was worrying quite a bit. The sun soon came up, and I still couldn't rest. I think the adrenaline rush I received from my anxiety helped keep me awake.

After being up for almost twenty hours in a row, worrying and praying, I received an email at about ten o'clock that morning. A brother in the church had written that he believed God wanted me to read Psalm 127:1-3: "Unless the Lord builds the house, they labor in vain who build it; unless the Lord guards the city, the watchman keeps awake in vain. It is vain for you to rise up early, to retire late, to eat the bread of painful labors; for He gives to His beloved even in his sleep."

Wow! It's like God had said, "Ron, I can see that you're losing sleep worrying about the church. I want you to know that if I don't build it, it isn't going to get built, and if I choose not to build it, no amount of worrying and fretting is going to help. But on the other hand, if I am going to take care of the church, you might as well go ahead and go to bed because your anxiety isn't going to help Me build it. Go to sleep, Ron, and let Me take care of things."

I love it when God gets that personal with me. Remember the words of Jesus in Matthew 4:4 when He said, "Man shall not live on bread alone, but on every word that proceeds out of the mouth of God."

Rhema is Greek for "word" in this verse, and it basically means "a personal word spoken from God"—one with our name on it. Jesus was saying that our lives will be guided by rhemas. If we don't line up our walk with these rhemas, then we will get off course and will not end up where God wants us to be.

DYING FROM BOREDOM

I am tired of all the theologians and scholarly Bible students who put so much dedication into destroying anything in today's society that speaks of the divine. Some of us are so afraid of taking the Bible at face value. We want to explain away everything that makes us uncomfortable or that stretches our American cultural thinking. I have lived my life in pretty much the same way Moses, Abraham, Jacob, Daniel, Elijah, Elisha, and Ezekiel lived theirs, and in much the same way the New Testament church lived their lives, including the Apostle Paul.

Yet today, the American church is anemic and apathetic. No wonder we're not winning the lost for the Lord. We are dying from boredom in the pew, thanks to many of our lukewarm yet sincere theologians and priests. One of the saddest things in the world is knowing that a super fabulous lifestyle awaits us, and yet three quarters or more of the Christian population aren't the least bit aware of this.

In 1997, I was diagnosed with leukemia and given four to five years to live. But God spared me. I believe He healed me, so I could live to write this book and tell others about the Lord's incredible gospel message. What do you think is behind verses such as 2 Timothy 3:5 where it speaks of people who are "holding to a form of godliness, although they have denied its power; avoid such men as these"? The word "power" in the Greek is *dunamis,* and it simply means, "inherent power."

More than a few overzealous, wildly imaginative men in the ministry have so totally turned us off to the truth that even *considering* talking to God and hearing His voice makes us shudder in fear of looking like fools. I had to overcome this fear myself, but the effort it took was so worth it.

What I have found is so real and authentic that no one needs to pump it up and cheerlead with the truth. We don't need any bells and whistles to make it more real. It stands on its own.

COINCIDENCE?

Sometimes I have one story of awe to tell during the week; other times I have two or three stories. Seldom are there none to share. You might think I have an overactive imagination or that what I've experienced is merely coincidence. Well, I firmly don't believe it's either. First, if these things just happened every month or two, then I might tend to agree with you, but they happen way too regularly to be coincidental. If you added up all the miraculous things that have happened in my life, the odds of them being coincidental would be highly remote. Second, the people in both the Old and the New Testaments had the same kind of miraculous occurrences I have experienced. Could it be that this is the normal way of life for all believers?

I have often wondered, what exactly caused the Church to start depersonalizing the walk we have with God? If you examine the lives of the Old Testament men and women who walked with God, you'll see that most every time God chose anyone to do anything for Him, He established a personal relationship with that person in order to guide and empower him or her to do His will. Also, in the New Testament, God was personally involved in the lives of most all the people whom He called into service.

Some say, "But we now have the written Word to guide us and lead us." And I agree with that wholeheartedly. I believe that the written Word is to be our primary source of wisdom from God, but that doesn't exclude the fact that He wants to be intimately involved with our lives. It's not difficult for us to see that while the Bible addresses many life issues, it also leaves many of them up for grabs. For example, the Bible doesn't specify who to marry, where to work, where to live, how to react to cancer, where to minister, who to stay away from, what to accept and what to reject, how to help people in need, and a myriad of other choices we have to deal with. The question we all have to answer is, does God want us to be on our own in relationship to all these very important decisions that come up in life? I seriously doubt it, especially being that this has never been His will at any other point in time throughout known history. From the very beginning, starting with Adam and Eve, God has desired to have a very personal relationship with man. Where in the Bible does it say this desire has changed? I know for a fact, without a shadow of doubt, it hasn't. God speaks to me and divinely guides me in life on a day-to-day basis. This has happened consistently and constantly for a period of over thirty years. AC (American Christianity) has a hard time accepting that fact, and even if they do say they agree, most often their lifestyle contradicts what American Christians profess to be true.

One of the words used in the Bible that describes the ministry of the Holy Spirit is the word *helper*. In other words, the Holy Spirit is the one who assists the believer in living a life that is pleasing to God. He wants to help us speak the right words, think the right thoughts, and do the right things. He's just waiting for us to call upon His power, yet very few Christians in today's church make a habit of calling upon the Holy Spirit for help, and most don't ever really acknowledge His existence in a practical way.

SHOCK-AND-AWE

When the Apostle Paul visited the church of Ephesus in Acts chapter 19, he asked them if they had received the Holy Spirit when they believed. But they had never heard of the Holy Spirit. As a result, he made them get re-baptized, and he refocused their attention on the indwelling Holy Spirit. Now let me ask you this same question: Did you receive the Holy Spirit *when* you believed?

The book of Acts is full of excitement with shock-and-awe types of events happening regularly. For example, in chapter one the disciples prayed over lots they were going to draw in order to choose an Apostle to replace Judas. They believed the Holy Spirit would make the lots fall on the right person. Now to most Christians in AC that kind of thing would insult their intelligence and would never, under any circumstances, be considered.

According to the second chapter of Acts, when the believers were in the Upper Room, "they were all filled with the Holy Spirit and began to speak with other tongues, as the Spirit was giving them utterance" (verse 4). It would be similar to being in a room full of people who got smashed with liquor and made fools of themselves. But on this occasion, instead of being made foolish, they were speaking in languages that they weren't supposed to be familiar with. It was utter chaos in an intriguing way. The party was anything but boring!

And then in the midst of the wild God-party, the Apostle Peter stood up and started preaching an amazing sermon to all the onlookers. We are told in Acts 2:37, "Now when they heard this, they were pierced to the heart, and said to Peter and the rest of the apostles, 'Brethren what shall we do?'" And then, in verses 41-47 of the same chapter, we are told that the early church was busy baptizing people and trying to keep up with all the new converts joining these groups. They were continually at each other's homes and at church listening to teachings, breaking bread, fellowshipping, and praying together. So many "wonders and signs" were taking place in their lives that they couldn't keep their jaws from constantly dropping in a spirit of awe.

For example, a spirit of giving had taken such a strong hold of the people that they were giving up some of their earthly possessions and using the money to help the poor. This generous spirit caused God to move so much more in their midst, and all they could do was praise the Lord continually for everything He was doing in their lives.

In Acts chapters 3, 4, and 5, the action continues. People are healed, people are arrested, and earthquakes come as a result of prayers. Angels showed up from time to time, and to top it all off, some who tried to get in the way of what God was doing were either prayed dead or prayed blind. Does this sound like what's going on in the average American church today? Is there any likeness at all? True, these are different times and cultures, but shouldn't there be some similarities?

No More Excuses

I know at our churches in California and Nevada, there are more similarities than not. We have been graciously blessed by God to see that we modern-day American Christians should live as the early believers did in the Middle East. The God we serve today is the same God of both the Old Testament and the early church, and His ways have not changed one bit, but the church has.

We have multitudes of believers created to live exciting, adventuresome lives, who are dying of boredom as they sit in their American churches week after week. And as a result, they end up going back to the same kind of lifestyle they were saved from. They not only don't understand their purpose in life, but they don't even understand the God of the Bible. They know very little about the working of the Holy Spirit, the existence of angels and demon spirits, and they couldn't hear God's voice if their life depended on it.

I have to wonder sometimes if the Christians in the early church would even recognize those of us in the American church as being legitimate believers. We can make up all kinds of excuses as to why we are like we are, but the fact remains that the early church was electrified in their love for God. They were consumed with their service for God, and they were amazed at His presence.

They had found to be true what Jesus described in John 10:10 where He said, "The thief comes only to steal and kill and destroy; I came that they may have life, and have it abundantly" (exceedingly, above the greatest abundance, super-abundantly). In other words, the life that Jesus predicted we would have, the early church found.

We can find that identical lifestyle today without all the embarrassing trappings often found in some church circles. Usually, when we hear of movements that resemble to some degree the characteristics of the early church in the book of Acts, they are almost always as fake as a three dollar bill and as goofy as can be. As a result, many of us have opted out for the boring and mundane over the fake and goofy. And we more than likely have thrown the baby out with the bath water.

THE REAL DEAL!

I suggest that in between some of the foolish and embarrassing going-ons we see operating in the Christian church today and the stuffy, boring services we attended with Aunt Jane when we were young, there is something very genuine and authentic. Let's not give up pursuing the real deal and settle for AC—American Christianity.

AC is a movement fueled and fed by many who are appointed instead of anointed. It's a movement that is doing more harm to our young people than it is doing good. It teaches those who are new to the faith (who come expecting something they are not going to get, namely a new life with a living, breathing God) that basically God doesn't exist. He's just a figment of society's wildest, hopeful imaginations.

AC gets these people to make commitments to the Lord, and then, when they discover they've been tricked into believing in a nonexistent god, they sometimes give up on their pursuit of the real God altogether. Many end up going back to the world from whence they came. And the sad part of the story is they will never try Him again. They've been there and done that!

We are subconsciously teaching our young people that prayer doesn't work, God doesn't care, and His Word is, well, just a bunch of words that really mean nothing. We are substantiating what the world has been trying to pound into their heads since they were born. We are playing right into the hands of the Hollywood jet set who try to continually influence our kids that the idea of a living, caring, all-powerful, personal God is a big joke. We are helping the enemy, and unless we wake up and rediscover the living God in the book of Acts, we might lose more than we wish to think.

Hang on and pray through each chapter of this book as we rediscover the God of the Jerusalem church.

Two

WHAT'S SO HARD ABOUT SERVING?

*Don't worry about doing something great.
Be great by doing what you can where God has
placed you. It will pay off after awhile.*

– PAUL ROBINSON

Contrary to opinion, God is not hard to please. At the end of every day, we should be able to come to Him and, after confessing our sins, lay our deeds of service before Him and receive several high-fives and accolades from Him.

One of the problems we have all likely faced at one time or another is trying to please someone who is so particular it seems as though nothing we do will ever be good enough. At some point, we usually throw our hands up into the air and give up. "What's the use?" we ask ourselves, and then we stop trying. This is the way many Christians see God and His demands upon our lives. But nothing could be further from the truth than this lie Satan has planted in our hearts.

Let me share a parable with you that helps drive home the nature of God's gracious demands upon our lives. In Matthew chapter 25, there is a parable concerning the talents. In this story, a man who was about to go on a journey called in his slaves and entrusted his possessions to them. He gave one five talents, to another he gave two, and to the last slave he gave one—"each according to his own ability; and he went on his journey" (verse 15).

WHO WOULD BE LEFT?

We all have been given different talents and skills. God doesn't want everyone to be preaching and traveling the world ministering the gospel. He doesn't ask everyone to write books. If we were all pastors or authors:

- There would be no one left in the church to help people find a seat, so that they could be comfortable to hear the morning message and allow God to heal their lives.
- There would be no one left who could greet people with a smile as they made their way onto the church grounds.
- There would be no one left to sell doughnuts and coffee, so that the youth group could raise enough money to sponsor poor kids to go to camp, where God could transform their lives.
- There would be no one left to print up the morning bulletins that inform people about all the healing ministries going on, no one to teach Sunday School, and no one to watch over the children in the nursery.
- There would be no one to make minor repairs on the church.

God wants someone sitting in the church pew, so that when people come to the altar and pour their hearts out to Him, there'll be caring individuals waiting to hug and comfort them with a word and a prayer.

Paul writes, in 1 Corinthians 12:14-18, 20-27 (Message):

A body isn't just a single part blown up into something huge. It's all the different-but-similar parts arranged and functioning together.

If Foot said, "I'm not elegant like Hand, embellished with rings, I guess I don't belong to this body," would that make it so? If Ear said, "I'm not beautiful like Eye, limpid and expressive; I don't deserve a place on the head," would you want to remove it from the body? If the body was all eye, how could it hear? If all ear, how could it smell? As it is, we see that God has carefully placed each part of the body right where He wanted it...

What we have is one body with many parts, each its proper size and in its proper place. No part is important on its own. Can you imagine Eye telling Hand, "Get lost, I don't need you?" Or, Head telling Foot, "You're fired, your job has been phased out?" As a matter of fact, in practice it works the other way—the "lower" the part, the more basic, and therefore necessary.

You can live without an eye, for instance, but not without a stomach. When it's a part of your own body you are concerned with, it makes no difference whether the part is visible or clothed, higher or lower. You give it dignity and honor just as it is, without comparisons. If anything, you have more concern for the lower parts than the higher.

If you had to choose, wouldn't you prefer good digestion to full-bodied hair? The way God designed our bodies is a model for understanding our lives together as church: every part dependent on every other part, the parts we mention and the parts we don't, the parts we see and the parts we don't. If one part hurts, every other part is involved in the hurt and in the healing. If one part flourishes, every other part enters into the exuberance. You are Christ's body—that's who you are! You must never forget this.

So we don't have to be something great to be something important. Every Christian has been intrinsically designed, so all

22

jobs in the kingdom can be accomplished.

THE TWO "FIELDS"

There are basically two parts to God's will for our lives. Let me explain. In 1 Corinthians 3:9 it says, "For we are God's fellow workers; you are God's field, God's building." The Greek word used here for field is *georgion,* and it means "cultivated field or farm." The idea is that the church is a field in which work has to be done.

As I've already explained, there are all kinds of jobs to be fulfilled in the church world. There are needs for ushers, greeters, bulletin makers, small group leaders, new convert follow-up people, Sunday school teachers, nursery workers, youth leaders, parking lot attendants, administrators, yard people, clean-up crews, and on and on. It would be ideal if all Christians belonged to a church and took it upon themselves to fulfill one of these jobs. If you haven't yet settled down in a home church, you should ask the Lord to help you find one and then become a worker in God's field, the church. Once you do this, you are in a position to receive heavenly rewards when you die. You can now live with a certain amount of confidence that you are pleasing God and fulfilling His will, and what a great feeling that is.

There's a second part of God's will, and that is we are to work in the other field called the "world field." In Matthew 13:38, it reads, "The field is the world." Here the Greek word used is *agros,* which basically means "a tract of land; countryside." And the Greek word for world is *kosmos,* meaning "the sum total of the material universe; the sum total of persons living in the world." In other words, the field of the world spoken of in Matthew is the one around us in which we live. We are to be workers in that field also. It includes our neighbors, coworkers, the people at Wal-Mart, the shopping mall, the PTA, and so forth.

Remember, the world includes both believers and non-believers. We work with both, and we live by both. Our job is to recognize that there is work to be done in the lives of the individuals with whom we come into contact every day.

People are in great need constantly. Depending upon the time and circumstance, we all go through periods of life when we need to be encouraged, loved, or given wisdom and reassurance. Sometimes we require help in the form of money or a helping hand to repair a water leak at home that we just don't know how to fix. There is rarely an occasion when we aren't living with some sort of need in our lives.

THE PERFECT PLAN

The Bible explicitly states that God wants to meet Christians' needs and also wants to show the world His great love for them. Acts 10:38 tells us, "You know of Jesus of Nazareth, how God anointed Him with the Holy Spirit and with power, and how He went about doing good and healing all who were oppressed by the devil, for God was with Him."

In His earthly ministry, Jesus taught and healed men, women, and children. He also encouraged and imparted the wisdom of God to them. John 1:1, "In the beginning was the Word, and the Word was with God, and the Word was God." The Greek word used here for "word" is *logos,* and it simply means, "God's idea or God's ideal plan." In other words, it says that in the beginning there was God's plan, that His plan was with God and was God.

In John 1:14, we also learn, "And the Word became flesh, and dwelt among us, and we saw His glory, glory as of the only begotten from the Father, full of grace and truth." So from the beginning, God had a message for mankind. He had a plan He wanted to share with those He'd created in His image—to include them.

Part of God's agenda was to make people members of His

family. However, in order to do this, He would have to first show them how much He loved and cared for them. So, in His earthly ministry, Jesus, the Word of God, came to this earth and did precisely what the Father wanted Him to do. He went around touching people with the love of God; He healed, taught, delivered, encouraged, and gave them hope. And then He died, rose again, ascended to heaven, and left His ongoing ministry to us. He gave us His Holy Spirit, so we would be empowered to continue His ministry to a lost and dying world.

When Jesus walked the dusty roads of Judea, He was confined to one earthly body, and He could only do so much. Therefore, He seized the opportunity to use His short earthly life to be a model and example for us to follow. What He did, we are supposed to do, and that's the idea behind what He said in John 14:12: "Truly, truly I say to you, he who believes in Me, the works that I do, he will do also; and greater works than these he will do, because I go to the Father."

We have been called to carry on the work of Jesus. It's the very reason we have been given the Holy Spirit. Today, far too many of God's people are living without purpose, and when you don't have purpose, you don't need power. When you don't have power, you become weak. And weak Christians sometimes backslide. Many of God's people are dying because of boredom and lack of purpose. They don't need the Holy Spirit like the people of the Bible did because they're not doing much for God.

"IF I ONLY HAD A BODY"

Many Christians today are like the Ephesians of the New Testament—not cognizant of the Holy Spirit. Paul asked them, "Did you receive the Holy Spirit when you believed?" And they replied, "No, we have not even heard whether there is a Holy Spirit" (Acts 19:2). Well, let me assure you there *is* a Holy Spirit. He guides us, convicts us when we veer off course, helps us remember things, encourages us, lets us know what to say in certain circumstances, empowers us, and works through us.

Sometimes I feel sorry for God because we are the only body He has in this world. There has to be times when the Father's heart breaks over someone who's in the hospital, hurting with no one to encourage him or her. As God looks down from heaven, His heart must ache. He probably thinks, "If I only had an earthly body, I would visit the hospital and bring that individual some flowers, and I would pray with them and show them God's love."

And likewise, when God sees young boys and girls without mothers or fathers, He must think, "If I only had a body, I would spend some time with these children and help them grow up with hope in their lives. I would take them to a football game or a shopping mall, and I would be a father to the fatherless and mother to the motherless."

I also believe God looks down at people confined behind bars and thinks, "If I only had a body, I would go to the prison and tell these prisoners, who think that society has given up on them and who are eaten up with guilt and remorse, that someone in heaven hasn't forgotten them. I'd show how I'm willing to forgive their trespasses, set them free from the guilt they live with day and night, and give them the hope of a better world to come."

He would help feed the children around the world who are dying of starvation, if He only had a body. He would stop by the homes of the depressed and suicidal, pray over them and set them free. On Christmas day, for the father who has lost his family and weeps because he can't see his children open their presents and give them a big hug, God would say to him, "I love you." He'd get on the phone and invite that man to come over to His house and be a part of His Christmas festivities. There is no way He would let this dad be alone in his pain.

To the little girl at school who has just been teased and taunted that her freckles are ugly and no one likes her, God would reach out with compassion and make her His best friend and tell her that she is beautiful, regardless of what anyone else says. He might even buy her a little gift at Wal-Mart just to show her how special she is. If He only had a body.

I could go on and on. There are many opportunities to be His hand extended throughout any given day. If we were only willing to be His body, what joy it would bring Him. And when God's happy with you, you will definitely know it (we will cover this in another chapter).

PILE ON THE ENCOURAGEMENT

One morning, when I awoke, Matthew 11:30 was on my mind. This is the passage of scripture where Jesus said, "For My yoke is easy and My burden is light."

I pondered Jesus' words until they became crystal clear to me. I concluded that a good father affirms his kids more than he punishes them. Well, if this is true of a caring earthly dad, then wouldn't this be even truer of our heavenly Father? He encourages more than He chastises and piles on the guilt. Yet where are the Christians who feel affirmed by God on a daily basis, who feel like God is giving them high-fives?

Let's return to the parable of the talents. The master of the household gave five talents to one slave, two talents to another and one to the third—each according to his own ability. Then the master went on his journey.

Verses 19-27 of Matthew 25 go on to say:

Now after a long time, the master of those slaves came and settled accounts with them. The one who had received the five talents came up and brought five more talents, saying, "Master, you entrusted five talents to me. See, I have gained five more talents."

His master said to him, "Well done, good and faithful slave. You were faithful with a few things, I will put you in charge of many things; enter into the joy of your master."

Also the one who had received the two talents came up and said, "Master, you entrusted two talents to me. See, I have gained two more talents."

His master said to him, "Well done, good and faithful slave. You were faithful with a few things, I will put you in charge of many things; enter into the joy of your master."

And the one also who had received the one talent came up and said, "Master, I knew you to be a hard man, reaping where you did not sow and gathering where you scattered no seed. And I was afraid, and went away and hid your talent in the ground. See, you have what is yours."

But his master answered and said to him, "You wicked, lazy slave, you knew that I reap where I did not sow and gathered where I scattered no seed. Then you ought to have put my money in the bank, and on my arrival I would have received my money back with interest."

In this account, we see something totally awesome about our God. The master didn't expect much from the slave who was only given one talent. He didn't expect the same amount of productivity as he did from the ones to whom he'd given the two and five talents. In fact, he told this last guy, "If you had only put my money in the bank so that it had accrued interest, I would have been happy. And you would have received a reward" (implied and stated in some translations).

In other words, God isn't the harsh taskmaster some of us depict Him to be. He says anything is better than nothing. *"My yoke is easy and My burden is light."*

SERVING IS SIMPLE

Think for just a moment about the twelve apostles Jesus chose. Not many of them would be considered by today's standards as men of great faith.

Take Andrew, for example. He never wrote a book in the Bible; he never performed a miracle. We don't see him praying for anyone who was supernaturally healed, and we know of no sermon he preached. The few times we read about him in scripture, all he's doing is introducing people to Jesus. I depict him as a real laid-back guy, chewing on a blade of grass, as he ponders the sayings of this man Jesus. Keep in mind that God knew what this guy was like before He chose him.

I can see Andrew kickin' back under a fig tree in the heat of a Galilean summer day. Along comes Phillip with some Greek believers. Phillip approaches Andrew and says, "Andy, these Greek guys want to see Jesus. Can you help them?"

Andrew gets up, still chewing on his blade of grass, and says, "Come this way, fellows." He then introduces them to Jesus, after which he resumes his position under the tree.

As far as we can tell, this is a big part of what Andrew did in scripture. He just introduced people to Jesus. Now, I'm sure he probably did more, but I think you get my idea.

We could illustrate the same with Bartholomew, Judas, Simon, and others. The point is, if we would just do small things for God each and every day, God would be happy. Remember what the Lord called the guy who squandered the one talent? Lazy. This slave figured that because the master was a hard man to please, he wouldn't try to please him at all. Because his perception of the master was wrong, he became slothful and did nothing.

God does expect service from us, but it is service we can so easily do.

"IT'S BEGINNING TO BE FUN"

Let's put this into practical terms. You get up on Monday morning and pray, "Oh God, anoint me with the Holy Spirit today to be Your body. I will be Your hands, feet, and mouth, and I will respond as You place people in my path and put them in my heart. Help me see what You want to do today, and give me a lot of help from the Holy Spirit, as I endeavor to be Your body in this mad and gone-crazy world. Amen."

On your way to work, someone comes to mind, so you pray for that person. Wow, you just served God one time, and it is only eight in the morning. Can't you just hear the Lord whistling and giving you high-fives in heaven?

Next, a fellow worker calls you on your cell phone, and in the course of conversation, she tells you about a problem she is having in her marriage. So you ask her, "Do you care if I say a short prayer for you?"

"No," she responds.

And so you pray, "God, help Sally forgive Mike for what he said, and show both of them that they need to start going to church and learn about Your great plan for marriage. Amen."

Now you've served God twice today, and it wasn't threatening to anyone. No one thought you were crazy or rejected you for doing what came so naturally. God is really, really happy with you.

Before you get to the office, a reckless driver cuts you off on the freeway, and you lay on the horn a bit too hard, and what you think for just a moment doesn't bring glory to God. But you confess it to the Lord and He forgives you right on the spot, and erases all condemnation. Praise God for His loving-kindness and forgiveness.

Once you arrive at the office, your boss calls you in and really lets you have it because yesterday's assignment wasn't done exactly the way he wanted. He could have been nicer, but no way, it just wasn't in him. "What a jerk!" you think, as you leave his office. But after a few minutes, you remember what you read in this book, and think, "Why let an opportunity like this pass without making God happy? It's beginning to be fun living this way."

So you pray, and ask God what Jesus would do in a situation like this. You wait a few minutes and mull over the situation, until a radical idea pops into your head: Why not buy the boss some Krispy Kreme doughnuts while you're out? After all, you're eating lunch today with Bob at the In & Out Burger, which is right by Krispy Kreme, and your boss always has said how much he likes those doughnuts. When you bring them, you could attach this note:

> *Sir, I'm so sorry for the shabby job I did yesterday on the project you gave me.*
> *I'm a Christian, and not only were you not pleased, but neither was God. As I prayed today, I believe the Lord put the desire in my heart to apologize to you and buy you these doughnuts. He must love you an awful lot. Again, I'm sorry.*
> *Enjoy!*

It's 1 P.M. and you've already served God three times. He must be so proud of you. The rest of the day is pretty normal, and you don't do much more for God. Not a lot of opportunities have come up to serve Him. But that night, as you kneel before your bed, you first confess your sins, and then thank the Lord that you were able to serve Him three times that day. And as you go to sleep, it's as if you can hear God whistle from heaven and shout out to you, "Good job, son!" And you drift into sleep with a smile on your face.

We serve a wonderful God—one who's not hard to please. *His yoke is easy and His burden is light.*

Super-Natural

If you feel far removed from God's presence, all you have to do is stir the Spirit up within you and pray a very simple prayer—

31

maybe something like this: "Lord, today I want to draw close to You, so You will draw near to me. I am sorry I've wandered so far off track. Please lay three people's names or faces upon my heart, and I will either call or write them a note after I pray for them. Thank You for hearing this prayer. In Jesus' name, amen."

Now if you do what you say you will do, I promise that God will start manifesting His presence in your life, and you will supernaturally be back in fellowship with Him. It's amazing how simple it really is.

Pay close attention to what Jesus says to us in John 7:17: "If any man is willing to do His (God's) will, he will know of the teaching, whether it is of God or whether I speak from Myself."

In other words, when you start doing God's will, the Lord will become so active in your life that you will definitely know you're not just keeping some man-made religious ritual, but that you are touching the presence and heart of God by your actions. You will sense such a spirit of peace and joy along with an adamant desire to not live in sin that the only way you can explain what you're experiencing is by attributing it to something in the supernatural realm.

The purpose of this book is to let you know that God's yoke is easy, and His burden is light. Jesus promises, "I came that they may have life, and have it abundantly" (John 10:10). Does this describe your life at the moment? If not, then maybe you should try taking a new approach to your spiritual walk. It works, I guarantee you.

NO MORE MAKE-BELIEVE SUITS

Manufacturers of polyester suits brag about the fact that their garments are pretty much wrinkle-free. They require little to no effort to maintain. We wear them, throw them back on the hanger, and they are good to go the next time we need them. If we're not careful, however, the suits can start smelling, and we may not even notice. While the majority of us no longer wear polyester suits, I'm not so sure that we don't want the polyester lifestyle in that we want life to be very low maintenance. We want a closet full of clothes that matches our every need. We want a yuppie suit, macho suit, sport suit, religious suit, cowboy suit, rich-and-famous suit, and maybe even a sexy suit. When an occasion arises where we need to look spiritual, we could just go to our closet, reach in and grab our religious garb and put it on. Right before we leave, we might stand in front of the mirror and practice some "Hallelujahs" and "Praise the Lords," and off we go wearing our make-believe suit.

Or, perhaps we want to look really cool and "with it," so we walk to our closet and pick out our yuppie suit or our rich-and-famous outfit—the one with little alligators or horses and men stitched on it. Before we leave the house, we put on our best costume jewelry (the stuff that looks real but isn't), and we practice our stride a bit. Then off we go to pretend as though we fit in with the cool jet set.

When Rodeo Week comes to town, we don't want to be left out, so we pull out our cowboy suit, boots, and hat. We have to walk a little differently with this gear on, so again we practice. We need to look as though we would actually know what to do with a cow if we had one in the backyard. We want to fit in, but not to the degree that we would really go to a dude ranch and use up some of our precious vacation time to learn about cows and horses.

Why go to all the trouble when we can fake it? And this is what we so often like to do. Why? Perhaps because faking it is much easier, and it requires so little time and effort. But we fail to see that it's all plastic—not *real!*

POWER, NOT PRETENSE

In chapter 34 of the book of Exodus, we're told that Moses was invited up to Mount Sinai to visit with God. After staying there with God for forty days and forty nights, Moses came back down to the people, and his face was glowing. Apparently, something marvelous happened to Moses after being in God's presence for all that time. A residue of God had attached itself to him, and you might say the people saw the Lord in him. They were shocked. But Moses came down from the mountain unaware that being in God's presence had made him look different.

Paul writes, in 2 Corinthians 3, that Moses was proud of the Lord's glory that shone on his face. Unfortunately, that glory soon began to fade. Day by day, it became less and less. Moses wanted to hide the fact that the glory, which had come from being in God's presence, was diminishing. Apparently, the only way Moses could receive any more of the glory was by getting back into the presence of God; however, it wasn't possible at that moment. As a result, Moses put on a mask. At least with a mask on, the people wouldn't be able to see the glory fading away.

In much the same way, you and I are daily invited into the presence of God to receive some of His glory, words, counsel, and power. If we spend time with Him, the results will be rather impressive. We will stop feeling the need to pretend that we are something we are not. We will even start losing the fear of being ourselves, of showing our weaknesses and needs. The glory of God that will be with us as a result of our closeness with Him will be so overpowering that the reality of our humanness will not be noticed.

There are times, when I'm preaching, I get so excited about what God has either done or said to me in the preceding week that in communicating it to thousands of people, I often use some bad grammar. I sometimes lose any form of dignity and sophistication a public speaker should have. I guess you could say that the excitement of the moment gets to me. Yet I sincerely believe that the impact of the God-story I tell makes much more of an impression than my lack of professionalism in sharing it.

Here's what I want you to see when I say that the yoke of the Lord is easy and His burden is light: I'm not implying that following the Lord requires absolutely no effort at all. To say something is easy doesn't mean that it is effortless. Our job is to get into the presence of God and spend time in His Word, daily. Once we make a practice of doing this, we will automatically find the power we need to live a godly life. We will no longer feel a desire to pull the various suits out of the closet. We will find in us the ability to relate to most everyone with a new spirit. God will be so strong in us that we won't feel the insecurity we felt before, nor will we feel the need to conform to the standards of the world. We will begin to sense a new calling to just simply be who God has called us to be. There's freedom in being filled with God's Spirit that I find hard to describe. It's a treasure you just have to experience for yourself.

Unlike Moses, I don't need to ever worry over losing God's glory because I know where to get more of it when I need it.

Polyester suits may be maintenance free, but we must always remember they are plastic and artificial. And if there's one thing this world doesn't need more of, it's plastic, fake Christians.

Three

YOUR AMAZING POTENTIAL

Lord we may know what we are,
but know not what we may be.
— WILLIAM SHAKESPEARE

There was a time when the nation of Israel was warring with the Philistines, and because they had suffered great loss in the first skirmish, they thought it would be wise to take the Ark of the Covenant with them in the second confrontation, so they brought it from Shiloh to the battlefield. Now, because God's presence resided with the Ark, the Israelites thought they would be assured a victory, but God did not want to be manipulated. The nation of Israel not only lost the battle but the Philistines captured the Ark of the Covenant and took it back to Ashdod, where they put it in the temple of Dagon, one of their heathen gods. Here's how the story picks up in 1 Samuel 5:3-4:

> *When the Ashdodites arose early the next morning, behold, Dagon had fallen on his face to the ground before the ark of the Lord. So they took Dagon and set him in his place again.*
> *But when they arose early the next morning, behold, Dagon had fallen on his face to the ground before the ark*

of the Lord. And the head of Dagon and both the palms of his hands were cut off in the threshold; only the trunk of Dagon was left to him.

Obviously, the power of God was so overwhelming in the heathen temple that the false god, Dagon, couldn't stand. I believe that God teaches us an important lesson in this story.

AVAILABLE STRENGTH

So many Christians go about dealing with sin in the wrong way. We try to defeat it by mustering up our own strength and overpowering it with self-determination. We hear a good sermon, get convicted, decide that we don't want to live for the devil any longer, and want to be pleasing to God. So we answer the call for rededication, and we are really sincere. On the way home, we even confess to our spouse, friend, or whoever is with us that we are finished with our sin. No more drugs, alcohol, or pornography. We have our minds made up.

But it's all short-lived. Why? Because we are dealing with sin in the wrong way. You might say we have the cart before the horse. We are trying to defeat sin by our own power, and that just won't work. In Philippians 4:13, Paul writes, "I can do all things through Him who strengthens me."

We are to do all things *through Him* and *His strength,* not our own. We have been made by God to be His conduits on the earth. The Creator has designed us in such a way that we make great channels for His Holy Spirit to speak through, love through, and act through.

Most everyone knows better than to grab hold of a live power line that has been knocked to the ground by a storm or some other natural disaster. We know that it's filled with the energy of electricity. The wire may just be made out of copper or aluminum and has no power in itself, but the power derives from what's racing through it—the electricity.

In the same way, when we are involved in the service of the Lord and are busy being a conduit for Him, the power of God surges through us constantly. As we give out words and prayers, we continually return to God to receive more words and prayers, because the first words caused things to happen. We then become somewhat like the power lines. We are filled with God's Holy Spirit, and wherever the Spirit is, there is strength.

This is one reason why, when we sit in church on Sunday morning, participate in worship, and then listen to the pastor preach, we feel so strong. Why? Because the Holy Spirit is moving through us as we release our worship and take in the preaching of God's Word. During these times, we usually aren't thinking about sinful acts. In fact, we feel about the strongest, spiritually speaking, that we can feel. I doubt many people are sitting in Spirit-filled churches thinking of how much they want to commit adultery or how they can't wait to go out and get drunk and cuss out their spouse. Usually, we're at our spiritual peak on Sunday mornings because we are in the Holy Spirit's presence.

SPONGES AND DUMP TRUCKS

In the story of the Ark of the Covenant and Dagon, God is teaching us that idols can't stand up in the same temple where the holy presence of God is abiding. When the Lord's presence is in the house, the idols start falling and crumbling. I continually tell Christians to get busy serving God with all their heart, soul, and strength and then watch what happens to the sins that have become so hard to defeat in their lives. I believe they will start falling and be destroyed. Instead of trying to deflect sin in our lives by gritting our teeth and overpowering it by sheer determination, we should make up our minds to start serving God as much as we can every day. We should exchange our R&B music and country tunes for praise and worship music and begin to do what I talked about in chapter two.

In a sense, we are much like sponges in the fact that we are called by God to live under His water faucet of truth and then wring ourselves out in the world by sharing our prayers, words, and encouragement. And after we wring ourselves out daily, we go back to God and get refilled.

I've also compared us to dump trucks in that daily we should get up and grab our Bible, an ink pen, and a pad, and sit before God. As we come before Him in our morning devotions, we should ask Him to lay people upon our hearts to pray for and also plant verses into our thinking. As we sense Him doing this, we should write these thoughts down and thank Him in childlike faith, then go on our way into the world to do our daily tasks. Then, as we encounter people in the course of our day, we are able to tell them that we prayed for them that morning. And we might share with them the verses that God laid upon our heart during our devotional time. We can let God do the rest. And believe me, that simple act alone can open up quite an opportunity for ministry.

The avenues for reaching the world are endless and mind boggling. And it's all so simple and non-threatening.

We are like dump trucks in that we get filled up during our morning time with God, and then throughout the day, we release the spiritual load. As we do, the Holy Spirit races through us like electricity. Our idols start falling because God is in the house. Our desire for sin lessens as we cultivate such a lifestyle.

CHANGE YOUR ENVIRONMENT

There's another interesting thought that parallels this and it comes out of Ephesians 6:10: "Finally, be strong in the Lord and in the strength of His might." In the Greek, this phrase means to "put oneself where the power of God is."

So how do we become strong in the Lord? By placing

ourselves in an environment where God's presence resides. Where is this? His presence lives in Bible studies, times of prayer, and Christian fellowship. The Word of God tells us that God inhabits the praises of His children.

When we go to a restaurant and sit down with a brother or sister and talk about the Lord, we feel strong and energetic. I tell people that when they are tempted to sin, instead of trying to fight off the temptation with self-determination, turn on some praise music in the car, sing along, and see what happens. Or call up a Christian brother or sister on the phone and ask for prayer, or start quoting the Word out loud. The results are amazing. There'll be a surge of strength and power from the Holy Spirit, and they will feel stronger than the temptation. Paul writes: "I can do all things through Him who strengthens me" (Philippians 4:13).

So often we neglect to go through God to get our power. We fail to see the truth of Ephesians 6:10, that we will be strong in the Lord when we put ourselves where God's power resides.

FIRST-HAND EXPERIENCE

It is vital that we deal with sin in our lives. When unconfessed sin is present, it blocks the flow of God's Spirit. We read in Isaiah 59:2, "But your iniquities have made a separation between you and your God, and your sins have hidden His face from you so that He does not hear."

Far too many Christians are living in unconfessed and unrepented sin. They live with iniquities because they don't believe God blesses His people, speaks to His people, and answers His people's prayers. Most men and women in AC (American Christianity) don't fully grasp what the Bible teaches. And their ignorance of the Word is costing them dearly. If they did gain an understanding, it would change the way they live, especially if they fully comprehend what is awaiting them if they deal with the sin in their lives and commit themselves totally to God's will and purposes.

There is so much the Word of God teaches that most people in AC don't comprehend. They've become content with just being religious Christians instead of committing themselves to becoming disciples or students of Jesus Christ and God's Word. I love the truth that Paul taught us in 2 Corinthians 4:6: "For God, who said, 'Light shall shine out of darkness,' is the One who has shone in our hearts to give the Light of the *knowledge* of the *glory* of God in the *face of Christ"* (emphasis mine).

To many, that verse contains a lot of verbiage, but let's break it down, so we can see its value. Look at the italicized words. First the word "knowledge" in the Greek is *gnosis,* which means "to have experiential knowledge or to know for yourself." And the Greek word for *glory* can mean "riches." So putting it all together, here's what the verse says: We have experiential knowledge about the riches of God by studying the person of Jesus.

COMMANDING THE CLOUDS

As I've studied the life of Jesus in the Bible, I have come to see how He used His power over the elements of nature when they stood in the way of getting God's will done. When the wind and waves threatened to keep the boat that He and the disciples were on from making it to the other side of the sea, He used His spiritual authority to rebuke them. The sea became still and calm.

I read what Jesus did, and I understood when He said, "Truly, truly I say to you, he who believes in Me, the works that I do, he will do also; and greater works than these will he do; because I go to the Father" (John 14:12).

Tell me what the church does with verses like these today. It's not difficult to see and understand what Jesus was saying to us. Because He used His authority over the elements of nature,

41

the next time I had a need in that area of my life, I decided to experiment and use my spiritual authority in the same way He did.

I have done this several times, and I'll give you one example. I was leading a group of people on a trip through the Holy Land, and on the last day it became very cloudy and overcast. It was an important day on the schedule for our group, as we were to visit many holy sites, including the Garden Tomb. When we got off the bus to begin our tour, it started raining rather heavily. And because none of us came prepared, we were all getting soaked. Some even cut up plastic bags to put over their heads!

We were at the Wailing Wall when it suddenly dawned on me that I didn't want everyone to get sick and be miserable the whole trip home, so I decided to put into practice what Jesus did in scripture.

I called several men together, and as we prayed, we spoke to the clouds. I took authority over the clouds and rain. In fact, I actually prayed that our heavenly Father would send angels and hold back the downpour until our tour was over. And guess what happened? It stopped raining within about thirty seconds of the prayer. And it never rained again for the whole day, not even once.

When we arrived at the airport at the end of the day, someone told me to look outside. When I did, I saw the rain coming down in sheets. What happened? You may say I got lucky and that it was mere coincidence. Let me again remind you that I have lived this life of faith for over thirty years, and these kinds of occurrences have happened far more often than I can count. I can't be lucky *all* the time!

On countless occasions, I've prayed for God to hold back the rain on days when I have conducted funerals for poor families who couldn't afford anything but an outside graveside service. I can't remember a single time God hasn't helped me in those endeavors.

SIGNS, WONDERS, AND YOU

Allow me to give you one more example. According to scripture, Jesus laid His hands on people and cast demons out of them. So, one day I decided to do the same with a young man who seemed very confused and heard voices in his head. And guess what? God honored His Word. The spirits began to shriek and carry on a conversation with me. I was totally blown away the first time, because I wasn't sure what to expect. It was just as Jesus said when He commissioned His disciples: "Go into all the world and preach the gospel to all creation. He who has believed and has been baptized shall be saved; but he who has disbelieved shall be condemned. These signs will accompany those who have believed: in My name they will cast out demons, they will speak with new tongues; they will pick up serpents, and if they drink any deadly poison, it will not hurt them; they will lay hands on the sick, and they will recover" (Mark 16:15-18).

Why is it we go to extremes to explain these verses away, instead of accepting them by faith? Notice the qualifier in Mark 16:17: *"And these signs will accompany those who have believed...."* It doesn't say the signs will accompany the twelve apostles or all the people until the New Testament age is over.

If we start picking and choosing which portions of the Word we will and won't believe, we will be treading on dangerous ground. Who has been given that kind of authority? Besides, I have conducted so many deliverances and taught others to do the same that it would be useless to even attempt to make me believe that casting out demons, healing the sick, and the ministry of miracles isn't for today.

Do you think God has stopped being concerned about people who are possessed by demons? Has He lost His compassion for them? Of course not! And yes, people are still occasionally possessed with evil spirits, just as they were in the day of Jesus. And they desperately need help.

Your Great Treasure

Let's go back again to 2 Corinthians 4:6-7. "For God, who said, 'Light shall shine out of darkness,' is the One who has shone in our hearts to give the Light of the knowledge of the glory of God in the face of Christ. But we have this treasure in earthen vessels, so that the surpassing greatness of the power will be of God and not from ourselves."

What is the treasure we possess? It's all the experiential knowledge we receive from studying the face and person of Christ and, as a result, practicing the way He lived. These truths we possess are invaluable to others and ourselves.

Still, you might be saying to yourself, *This kind of stuff just doesn't happen. I don't believe it at all.* That's the problem. You don't believe it, and if you don't, then possibly it won't happen for you, because you must have faith in God's Word in order for it to work.

AC likes to play it safe. We say that we can't afford to make *God* look bad, but is that honestly our real concern? Or is it that we don't want to make *ourselves* look bad? Are we afraid to step out in faith on God's Word?

One of the best things I ever did for myself was to come to a place where I didn't care what other people thought. I just want to do God's will. Have I made a lot of mistakes along the way? You bet I have, but I wouldn't trade my experiences with God and my relationship with Him for some of the mundane, lifeless relationships I see every day.

The "Empty" Factor

If we are going to understand the life of Christ properly, we must understand Philippians 2:5-8: "Have this attitude in yourselves which was also in Christ Jesus, who, although He existed in the form of God, did not regard equality with God a thing to be grasped, but emptied Himself, taking the form of a bond-servant, and being made in the likeness of men. Being found in appearance as a man, He humbled Himself by becoming obedient to the point of death, even death on a cross."

Notice the word "emptied" in verse seven; it's the word *kenoo* in the Greek, and it means the opposite of "to fill,"—basically "to empty."

At His incarnation, Jesus laid aside the privileges of power, authority, and rights He had while in the Godhead, yet He still remained God in essence and character. In verse seven, the word *existed* means that He continued to be that which He always was. Although He was still God in His nature, He did not regard equality with the Father a thing to be grasped. He made a decision to lay aside the privileges He has as God, so He could become as much like mankind as possible. He wanted to be able to identify with all our sorrows and temptations. He didn't want any advantages that we don't possess.

Hebrews 2:18 states, "For since He Himself was tempted in that which He has suffered, He is able to come to the aid of those who are tempted." And in Hebrews 4:15, we read, "For we do not have a high priest who cannot *sympathize* with our weaknesses, but One who has been tempted in all things as we are, yet without sin" (emphasis mine).

In the Greek, the word *sympathize* means to have compassion for. There is no way Jesus could feel compassion for us without feeling the full impact of sinful temptation. And He couldn't know the full impact without emptying Himself of all the privileges He had in the Godhead. Jesus felt the full weight of mankind's struggles with temptation, yet He did not sin.

John 1:1 tells us, "In the beginning was the Word *(logos),* and the Word was with God, and the Word was God." This refers to Jesus, but it goes on to say, in verse 14, "And the Word became flesh, and dwelt among us..." The Greek word for *flesh* means "the earthly nature of a man apart from divine influence."

THE SOURCE OF YOUR POTENTIAL

There's one more point you must understand or you'll totally miss one of the most important things in the New Testament. Jesus, while in His earthly ministry, could not do miracles or anything supernatural until He was endowed with the Holy Spirit at His baptism. Why? Because He had emptied Himself and needed the Holy Spirit to accomplish His ministry. This is why we need the indwelling of the Holy Spirit to do the work God has called us to do.

What Jesus did in His earthly ministry, He did by the power of the indwelling Holy Spirit, nothing more and nothing less. So, in essence, everything Jesus did while He was in His earthly role, we have the potential of doing, because we have the same Holy Spirit that resided in Jesus' body.

And again, this idea fits wonderfully with what Jesus said, as recorded in John 14:12, that we would do the same works He did. Our potential in Christ is unlimited, yet in AC we have believers sitting around bored stiff with their lives. Now granted, we must acknowledge the fact that Jesus did and said only what the Father did and said. Likewise, we can do only those things that God the Father shows or tells us to do. This is where God's voice comes into play. Jesus spent a lot of time praying and communing with His heavenly Father for many reasons, but primarily so that He would know the Father's will.

We need to also pray to know the Father's will since we are to carry on the ministry of Jesus on this earth. He told His disciples that it was to their advantage that He go away. How could it be to their benefit to lose the Son of God walking among them, unless Jesus was referring to the impact of having 120 people walking around with much of the same authority and potential power that He had?

A LIFELONG COMMITMENT

Let's go back to the Word of God, our source of revelation and guidance. Second Peter 1:4 records something that should be of great interest to us: "For by these He has granted to us His precious and magnificent promises, so that by them you may become partakers of the divine nature."

Most people in the 21st century church fail to understand that we've been both called and anointed to be mirrors of Jesus here on earth. Once you realize the enormous responsibility of this calling, it's very sobering to say the least. It implies a lifelong commitment, along with our dependence on the Holy Spirit to develop the qualities and characteristics of Jesus in us.

Our heavenly Father searches the earth for people who are endeavoring to pattern their lives after His Son. Once He finds them, the Bible says that He will bless, prosper, and help them. God greatly supports those who forsake their own will to do His.

Four

TURNING TRIALS INTO TRIUMPHS

*A faith that hasn't been
tested, can't be trusted.*

— ADRIAN ROGERS

One of the many things I like so much about the Word of God is that it doesn't sugar-coat life for us. God apparently felt no need to win converts to Himself by luring them into His kingdom through promises of an earthly life of eternal bliss, absent from the day-to-day problems everyone else faces.

God addresses life head on, and when a person has the Lord in his heart and is in fellowship with Him on a daily basis, he will always have whatever he needs to face anything that life might throw his way. This includes the need for power, love, consolation, strength, wisdom, encouragement, and more.

The Bible strongly teaches that God is more than enough. In fact, one of the Old Testament names for God is I AM, or "I am all that my people need when they need it."

Jesus echoed this thought in John 14:6 when He declared, "I am the way, and the truth, and *the life.*" In other words, He is our source of life; we need no more than Him to face any crisis or obstacle.

A DEATH-AND-BEYOND EXPERIENCE

The story of Paul's thorn in the flesh, in 2 Corinthians 12, illustrates this idea in a very poignant way. The chapter starts out telling us that the Apostle Paul had a death-and-beyond experience. More than likely the stoning he received in Acts chapter 14 resulted in a temporary death situation, where Paul actually left his body, entered heaven, and saw things that were beyond human description—things too marvelous and lofty to explain in human words.

Here's what we are told in 2 Corinthians 12:7, "Because of the surpassing greatness of the revelations, for this reason, to keep me from exalting myself, there was given me a thorn in the flesh, a messenger of Satan to torment me—to keep me from exalting myself."

Let's analyze this verse for a moment. As disciples of Christ, we are admonished to be pupils or students of the Word. The first question we want to ask ourselves is, "Who didn't want Paul exalting himself?" Was it Satan or God? Well, I think the answer is both Satan and God.

Satan didn't want Paul going around boasting how great heaven was and convincing people it was a real place they could look forward to going to someday. The devil certainly didn't want Paul any more on fire than he already was. He desired to keep Paul discouraged, if he could, just like he wants to keep us doubting and unsure. If a person gets on fire for God and stays that way, people will come to watch the flame, so Satan didn't want Paul exalting himself.

But more so, God didn't want Paul boasting because the Lord is unable to use a prideful person—someone who thinks too highly of himself. Many teach that we have a self-esteem problem in society today. In my opinion, just the opposite is true—we think too highly of ourselves. Paul wrote: "For through the grace given to me I say to every man among you not to think more highly of

49

himself than he ought to think" (Romans 12:3).

Both James and Peter told us that God opposes the proud of heart. For example, in James 4:5-6 we read, "Or do you think that the Scripture speaks to no purpose: 'He jealously desires the Spirit which He has made to dwell in us?' But He gave a greater grace. Therefore it says, *'God is opposed to the proud, but gives grace to the humble"* (those who see a constant need for God).

HOW STRONG ARE YOU?

The idea presented in scripture is that God desires His Spirit to dwell in us and feel at home in our bodies. But if we have a prideful or arrogant nature, then the Holy Spirit will not be able to enter into our lives and be comfortable. He comes as our helper, not the doer, and He is only at home in us when we let Him do His divine work of helping us through life.

When was the last time you called upon the Holy Spirit to guide and assist you in some area? Your dependency upon God makes Him feel at home in your body, and this is why it says in verse 6 that God gives grace to the humble.

It is not God's plan for us to grow in strength the longer we live. On the contrary, we are to remain cognizant of our weakness throughout our entire life. Then we will see our constant need for the Lord, and as a result, we will remain daily at His altar. We need God and the power His Holy Spirit gives every waking hour.

How strong do you think you are?

- Are you strong enough to fight off temptation when you click on the Internet?
- Are you strong enough to be bold and witness to the grocery store cashier if God should open a door for you to do so?
- Are you strong enough to turn the channel on the television set when, right in the middle of a really good movie, a scene appears that is totally contrary to the fruit of the Holy

Spirit and moves the flesh to desire things it should not have?

• Are you strong enough to stop and pray with your spouse right in the middle of a very heated argument, one in which your pride has totally been insulted?

• Are you strong enough to say you are sorry to a very defiant child who disrespected you to such a point that it caused you to react in a way you know you shouldn't have?

• Are you strong enough to control each and every thought that comes into your mind?

• Are you strong enough to control your tongue when you are visiting with friends and the opportunity to throw out a little bit of gossip presents itself?

If you couldn't answer many of these questions with a resounding yes, then just maybe you need the Holy Spirit more than you think you do. Perhaps you need to make Him feel more wanted in your life by requesting His help several times a day. Oh, how we have strayed from the elementary teachings of the Word of God.

TAKE THE TEST

We all need God's help much more than we think we do. If you're still not convinced, try taking 1 Corinthians 13 and inserting the name of Jesus in the place of *love*. You will quickly see that the words *love* and *Jesus* are interchangeable.

Take your own name and exchange it with the word *love* and see how far you get. Read it out loud: "*Love* is patient, *love* is kind and is not jealous; *love* does not brag and is not arrogant, does not act unbecomingly; it does not seek its own, is not provoked, does not take into account a wrong suffered, does not rejoice in unrighteousness, but rejoices with the truth; bears all things, believes all things, hopes all things, endures all things. *Love* never fails" (verses 4-8).

How did you do? Maybe we should call upon God's Spirit to help us more. Also in 1 Peter 5:5-6, we are told basically the same thing: "You younger men, likewise, be subject to your elders; and all of you, clothe yourselves with humility toward one another, for *God is opposed to the proud, but gives grace to the humble.* Therefore humble yourselves under the mighty hand of God, that He may exalt you at the proper time."

Peter tells the young men to put themselves in a position of submission under the elders of the church. The elders are wiser and have been around longer, and they can offer spiritual guidance that will be useful when hard times hit. Again, this verse points out our need for help by others.

God put us in the body of Christ where no single individual member can make it without the other parts of the body. My hand wouldn't do a lot of good without the arm. The eyes need the head and the toes need the feet.

After telling us that we aren't strong enough to make it alone, Peter emphasizes the point further by saying, "Clothe yourselves with humility toward one another." We must learn to see the other person as valuable, with much to contribute.

We need God, His power, and His people to fulfill His plan in our lives.

THE SOURCE OF THE PROBLEM

Remember Paul's thorn in 2 Corinthians 12:7? God did not want Paul to think of himself as a Superman-type of Christian who knew all the answers because of the revelation he'd received while having a death-and-beyond experience. The word *revelation,* according to Webster's Dictionary is defined as, "a revealing, or disclosing, of something; God's manifestation of the divinity or of the divine will to humanity."

We can only imagine what God revealed to Paul while he was caught up into heaven. Maybe He unveiled what the apostle's position would be in eternity if he fulfilled God's will while on earth. Perhaps God showed Paul all the planets he would be over if he remained faithful to God's calling on his life. Who knows? Paul may have seen the seraphim and cherubim—maybe his own guardian angel. Whatever Paul saw and heard, it brought with it a natural tendency toward arrogance and self-exaltation, and God had to counteract that temptation with something that would keep Paul's eyes focused on his need for God's strength and help. God allowed certain circumstances to come into Paul's life that kept him humble.

Scripture tells us that whatever that thorn was, it had demonic connotations attached to it. Down through the years, many theologians and commentaries have discussed and debated how this demonic force manifested itself. Some say it was an eye disease that bothered him and kept him humble. Others, for some odd reason, believed Paul had a tendency to be plagued with epileptic convulsions. I don't mean to sound as if I know more than these great men, but to me it's very simple to figure out how the devil's messenger manifested himself in Paul's life. All we have to do is go back to the chapter before this one and read 2 Corinthians 11:23-30:

Are they servants of Christ?—I speak as if insane—I more so; in far more labors, in far more imprisonments, beaten times without number, often in danger of death. Five times I received from the Jews thirty-nine lashes. Three times I was beaten with rods, once I was stoned; three times I was shipwrecked, a night and a day I have spent in the deep.

I have been on frequent journeys, in dangers from

rivers, dangers from robbers, dangers from my country-men, dangers from the Gentiles, dangers in the city, dangers in the wilderness, dangers on the sea, dangers among false brethren; I have been in labor and hardship, through many sleepless nights, in hunger and thirst, often without food, in cold and exposure.

Apart from such external things, there is the daily pressure on me of concern for all the churches. Who is <u>weak</u> without my being weak? Who is led into sin without my intense concern? If I have to boast, I will <u>boast</u> of what pertains to my <u>weakness</u>.

I've underlined the words "boast," "weak," and "weakness," so you can more easily understand the passage in 2 Corinthians 12. I suggest that many, if not all of the beatings, labor, stonings, shipwrecks, dangers from robbers, hardships, and the daily pressures of concern for the churches, were demonically linked trials. At least, if they weren't caused by demons, they were exploited by them. The effect of these trials and tribulations made Paul feel like there were demonic forces beating on his flesh and trying to destroy him. And so he went to God in prayer to ask Him to do something about these awful heartaches. He wanted God to override and stop them from happening.

Read 2 Corinthians 12:8: "Concerning this I implored the Lord three times that it might leave me." He was tired of having to put up with all these demonically linked harassments. But God said something that forever changed Paul's life and the way he saw trials and tribulations. In verse 9 we read, "And He has said to me, 'My grace is sufficient for you, for power is perfected in weakness.' Most gladly, therefore, I will rather boast about my weaknesses, so that the power of Christ may dwell in me."

Teleioo is the Greek word used for "perfected" in verse 9. It means "to make perfect, complete; to carry through completely, to accomplish, finish, bring to an end."

God explained to Paul, "I'm not going to take these trials out of your life. They serve a purpose. They keep you at the altar, and keep you close to Me. But here's the deal, whenever these problems appear, if you will come and seek Me, I will tell you how to respond. And if you will do and say what I tell you to, you will find My strength and power becoming greater than the trial."

To us these may be just words, but to Paul this was divine revelation that forever changed his life. Compare this to what he said in 2 Corinthians 11:30: "If I have to boast, I will boast of what pertains to my weakness." I believe our understanding of this will dramatically transform us, too.

God promises, "What I will do in the midst of the trial will be so great that people will have to know there's a God in heaven. I will use these trials to bring glory to Myself. In fact, I have already given you all the authority and power you need to turn any trial into a triumph."

The gospel singer André Crouch wrote, "Through it all, through it all, I've learned to trust in Jesus, I've learned to trust in God. Through it all, through it all, I've learned to depend upon His Word. If I never had a problem, I wouldn't know my God could solve them, I wouldn't know what faith in Him could do."

Paul was ecstatic. What the Lord told him made sense. Look at 2 Corinthians 12:10: "Therefore I am well content with weaknesses, with insults, with distresses, with persecutions, with difficulties, *for Christ's sake;* for when I am weak, then I am strong."

Paul basically expressed, "Now when problems come my way for the sake of Christ, I get all excited because I know if I look to God, He'll manifest Himself in the trials, and everyone will see His great and mighty power and be amazed."

WHY STAY STRESSED?

Our problems are nothing more than opportunities for God to

reveal Himself in our lives one more time. The Father is faithful to His children when they suffer and go through difficult times. As I stated at the beginning of this chapter, believers face the same kinds of trials and problems as the nonbelievers. The only difference is that God accompanies us through them, and when He is by our side, it's going to make a world of difference.

Are you finding God in the midst of your problems? Or are you even looking for Him? Let me reinforce this idea even more by drawing your attention to 2 Corinthians 2:12-16. Let's renew our minds, so we can think like the Apostle Paul and Jesus did.

> *Now when I came to Troas for the gospel of Christ and when a door was opened for me in the Lord, I had no rest for my spirit, not finding Titus my brother; but taking my leave of them, I went on to Macedonia.*
>
> *But thanks be to God, who always leads us in triumph in Christ, and manifests through us the sweet aroma of the knowledge of Him in every place. For we are a fragrance of Christ to God among those who are being saved and among those who are perishing; to the one an aroma from death to death, to the other an aroma from life to life. And who is adequate for these things?*

I want you to be all jazzed about what Paul has just told us. He starts out by telling us that he went to Troas for the gospel's sake. In other words, he went because of God. When God calls you to do something for Him, He will always be faithful to you and be there with you in a special way. After all, you are tending to His business. He's like any good, earthly father—but much greater. The Bible calls God our heavenly Father for a reason. God specifically chose the term to help us understand His relationship with us.

When Paul arrived at Troas he couldn't find Titus, who was supposed to meet him there, and he panicked. What happened to

Titus? Paul's imagination began to run wild. Was he hurt, dead, or did he even arrive there in the first place? How could he make it without Titus? Paul went into an all-out worry mode, much like many of us do today. But in the process of wringing his hands and taking ulcer medicine, a thought occurred to Paul, which came out of nowhere: "But thanks be to God, who always leads us in triumph in Christ" (verse 14).

He probably thought, "Duh! Why am I sitting here stressing out? Doesn't God always lead us in the way of triumph? Don't we know that the Lord causes all things to work together for good to those who love God, to those who are called according to His purpose (see Romans 8:28)?"

It suddenly dawned on Paul that every time he experienced a trial, God eventually worked it into some kind of triumphant situation. God used the trial for His glory. He is not sporadic, but faithful all the time.

WHAT ARE YOU LOOKING FOR?

How about you? Has your problem turned positive yet? If not, then God's not done working in your situation, so don't insert a period where God wants to put a comma.

You might say, "But Ron, I just don't believe that God can turn this trial around." Then He probably won't, at least not for you, because God moves in our lives when we believe and have faith in Him. So change your attitude and decide to believe that God's Word is truer than what circumstances are saying to you. Believe in God, and you'll see His Word perform miracles in your life. Why do you think Jesus went around all the time telling people, "Your faith has made you well," or "Let it be to you according to your faith?" We need to begin to believe in God the way Paul believed in Him.

I've often said that a person will see what they're looking for. If you place your faith in God and believe in Him, His goodness, and His faithfulness at all times, then I guarantee you will never be disappointed. The Lord wants to do something amazing in the midst of your circumstance today. Trust Him and look for Him to manifest Himself and intervene in your situation, and He will. God doesn't lie. His Word is one hundred percent true.

Hebrews 13:5-6 tells us: "For He Himself has said, 'I will never desert you, nor will I ever forsake you,' so that we confidently say, 'The Lord is my Helper, I will not be afraid. What will man do to me?"

Look for God in your trial today. Tell Him that you will not stop searching for Him until you find Him, because you know He's there with you.

In Proverbs 8:17, the Lord says, "I love those who love Me; And those who diligently seek Me will find Me."

HEARING FROM HEAVEN

God is showing up all around us every day, but we're just not seeing Him. Many of us are like the Pharisees and Scribes in that we are always looking for the Messiah to arrive, yet fail to recognize Him when He stands right in front of us!

So many of us are not conditioned to see Jesus in the midst of a TV movie. God forbid we see a revelation of Him and hear His voice speak to our hearts when we read a story in the *Reader's Digest.* Few of us hear God's voice when He decides to tell us something through an eight-year-old child. We don't always recognize that our heavenly Father is trying to speak a very crucial word to us when we read scripture in our daily time of devotion.

Do we ever hear God in a song on the radio? Do we ever expect to hear God in the stillness of our souls when we sit quietly before Him in the backyard before retiring to bed? Do we hear Him say things to us through the conversations we have daily with the people with whom we work?

On dozens of occasions, I have told nonbelievers that God just spoke a word through them to me. I tell them that I heard God in something they said.

I love Proverbs 3:5-6: "Trust in the Lord with all your heart and do not lean on your own understanding. In all your ways acknowledge Him, and He will make your paths straight."

I guess the opposite of this is also true, that if we fail to acknowledge God in everything, then our paths will become crooked and rugged.

Problems surface in the life of a servant of God just like anyone else's, but the Lord uses our problems to glorify Himself or make Himself exalted in other people's eyes. God wants men and women to see that He's real—this is one of His primary objectives in saving us. He wants to show others how much He loves mankind.

Does your life make those around you think about the Lord? If someone never read the Bible but only observed your life, what would their opinion be of God?

AN OBJECT LESSON

I love the story which tells how a great man of God awoke one morning to see his wife standing in front of the bedroom mirror all dressed in black. Wiping the sleep out of his eyes, he asked her, "Who died?"

Without hesitation, she said, "Oh, you haven't heard? God died."

"That's impossible," he replied. "Totally absurd. How could you believe such a lie?"

She sharply responded, "Because of the way you have been living, I thought He had died."

Wow! What an object lesson that must have been!

Paul taught us how God wants to work in our trials until He turns them into triumphs. As Christians we should never let any

59

problem defeat us. We should keep seeking God until He turns the situation around.

In 2 Corinthians 2:14, Paul tells us that as a result of God showing up in our lives, we become "the sweet aroma of the knowledge of Him in every place." Because of what God is doing in us, people smell God's fragrance on our very being. Wherever we go, men and women recognize God's presence with us. We become a witness of His reality.

Paul continues in verses 15 and 16 that for people who don't want Christ, we become an aroma of death for them, but for those who love God, we become an aroma of life. The reality of God's presence in our life is encouraging to some and discouraging to others.

FOUR REASONS FOR TRIALS

So, why does God allow trials to come into the lives of Christians? Let me suggest there are four basic reasons.

Reason #1: God allows trials to get us to change our behavior.

If we are traveling down Road B, and God wants us over on Road A, He might allow things to get rather bumpy on Road B. Take the Old Testament story about a man named Balaam. One day, Balaam was traveling down a road that God didn't want him on, so God caused his donkey to start veering off the path. And each time this would happen, Balaam would beat the animal and get it back on the road. The donkey was obviously not cooperating with its master for reasons that were divine, but Balaam didn't recognize the significance behind it. He kept insisting that they stay on the wrong road.

When things aren't going smoothly, we need to stop and ask the Lord whether we are on the right path. Some of us, like Balaam, just keep blindly forging ahead without ever consulting our heavenly GPS system.

Another illustration of this is found in Acts 16 when the Apostle Paul wanted to preach the Word in Asia, but some events happened that hindered him from going there. He then attempted to journey into Bithynia, but God caused certain things to occur that prevented him from going there, as well.

Paul had to be frustrated. It seemed so logical that those were the right roads to travel down, but God had different plans.

Acts 16:9-10 tells us: "A vision appeared to Paul in the night: a man of Macedonia was standing and appealing to him, and saying, 'Come over to Macedonia and help us.' When he had seen the vision, immediately we sought to go into Macedonia, concluding that God had called us to preach the gospel to them."

God had a different route for Paul to follow. Trials can be used to make us uncomfortable so that we will get to the place where God wants us to be.

Reason #2: God allows trials to test the genuineness of our faith.

Read 1 Peter 1:6-7: "In this you greatly rejoice, even though now for a little while, if necessary, you have been distressed by various trials, so that the proof of your faith, being more precious than gold which is perishable, even though tested by fire, may be found to result in praise and glory and honor at the revelation of Jesus Christ."

Every Christian must go through difficulties to prove to himself or herself, to God, and to the world that he or she is the real deal. Remember Job? How did he respond in the midst of a terrible ordeal?

Practically everything I've taught you in this book, so far, comes together in the Book of Job. First, he goes through some horrendous moments just as the Apostle Paul did, which were from the hands of Satan. The book of Job tells us that the devil was the one behind the tragedies in Job's life.

Job 1:8-12 says:

> *And the Lord said to Satan, "Have you considered My servant Job? For there is no one like him on the earth, a blameless and upright man, fearing God and turning away from evil."*
>
> *Then Satan answered the Lord, "Does Job fear God for nothing? Have you not made a hedge about him and his house and all that he has, on every side? You have blessed the work of his hands, and his possessions have increased in the land. But put forth Your hand now and touch all that he has; he will surely curse to Your face."*
>
> *Then the Lord said to Satan, "Behold, all that he has is in your power, only do not put forth your hand on him."*
>
> *So Satan departed from the presence of the Lord.*

Satan used his power to destroy everything precious in Job's daily existence. He shattered his homes, slaughtered his livestock, destroyed his livelihood, killed all his children and servants, and afflicted his body with disease and pain. Now, don't you think Job was wondering where God was during all these calamities? Did the Lord even care? He seemed to be nowhere in sight, but did that cause Job to stop believing in Him? Nope, not at all. Job said, "Naked I came from my mother's womb, and naked I shall return there. The Lord gave and the Lord has taken away. Blessed be the name of the Lord" (Job 1:21). Verse 22 adds, "Through all this Job did not sin nor did he blame God."

Wow! He was the real deal. He wasn't just giving God lip service to see what he could get out of it. No jailhouse conversion here. And then further on, in 2:10, after his wife told him that he needed to curse God and die, he said, "You speak as one of the foolish women speaks. Shall we indeed accept good from God and not accept adversity?' In all this, Job did not sin with his lips."

Far too many give their lives to God for all the wrong reasons. Many are in crisis and want God to do something for them like repair their marriage, restore their health, or get them out of jail. Their desire to follow God isn't sincere. It is through adversity that we can see who has an honest motive and who doesn't.

Sincere believers have their character shaped and deepened through life's hard knocks. They learn to love deeper and forgive completely; they learn the importance of giving grace to others; they can relate to people's pain.

Regarding Job, we are told in 42:1-17 that God turned his trial into a triumph. This is what God always has done and will continue to do when we keep our eyes focused on Him and our faith alive with a spirit of expectancy. In verse 10, it reads: "The Lord restored the fortunes of Job when he prayed for his friends, and the Lord increased all that Job had twofold." Verses 12-13 continue: "The Lord blessed the latter days of Job more than his beginning; and he had 14,000 sheep and 6,000 camels and 1,000 yoke of oxen and 1,000 female donkeys. And he had seven sons and three daughters."

What victory—and it came after the valley!

It is said that by affliction, the Lord separates the sin that He hates from the soul that He loves. God does His finest work in our lives in the midst of trials. In my bout with leukemia, I was forced to go deeper with God than ever before. You can read about it in my book *Conspiracy of Silence.*

Reason #3: God allows trials to come into our lives, so the world can see that God is real.

You can apply many things we have discussed to this point. When God heals a fractured marriage, the world stands up and takes notice. And when the world sees a person go through a battle with cancer and he or she keeps on rejoicing, the world pays attention. And when an individual loses a job and continues to smile, it arouses the world's curiosity.

Reason #4: God allows us to go through trials, so we can relate to others who go through similar problems.

Being able to identify with others is a powerful tool in the hands of God. On many occasions, I've sat and wept with people who are going through valleys in their lives, because I've been there, and I know firsthand some of the pain they are experiencing.

I think about the story of the Good Samaritan. The Samaritan people were considered half-breeds because they weren't pure Jews. Because of this, they were often ostracized and treated badly by others. So it comes as no surprise that when the Good Samaritan was traveling down the road from Jerusalem to Jericho and saw a man who had been beaten and stripped by robbers lying beside the roadway, he had compassion on him.

All the religious folk were not concerned about his condition. They just passed him by. But the Samaritan felt empathy for him and stopped to help. Why? Because he knew exactly what it felt like to be taken advantage of and ignored by other people. He related to the hurt that the wounded man felt and ministered out of that fellowship.

He had been where that man was.

REJOICE, PRAY, ENDURE

If you are going to be an effective servant of God, you must understand why trials come into the life of a believer and what to do with them when they arrive.

First, rejoice in your trial. The books of both James and Peter tell us to do this. Why? Because rejoicing speaks a loud message to God, the people in the world, and even to ourselves that we believe our God is in control of our lives. We delight in His great love for us and in the knowledge He will help us get through any problem. To rejoice is to be proactive in our faith. I believe it releases faith.

Second, we need to spend time praying over the trial to see if it has come because of something we are doing that isn't right. We need to be open and transparent before God and ask Him to reveal whether what we are going through is a form of divine discipline.

Hebrews 12 teaches that God disciplines us when we involve ourselves in sinful activity. The people of God were exiled to foreign nations because they had lived in sin and refused to repent of their evil ways. If a trial surfaces as a result of the Lord's divine discipline, relief will come only through repentance.

Third, after rejoicing and praying, we simply need to endure the trial, let it run its course, and continue doing whatever God tells us to do. We should keep busy and not focus on the situation. Instead, we should turn our attention to all the good things that are happening in our lives. If we wait on God, He will see us through anything. We need to let the trial produce a deeper and more mature character.

THE GOOD ABOUT THE BAD

I love the phrase in the Bible that says, "And it came to pass..." Trials do come to an end. It might not seem that way at the time, but they do. The pain doesn't remain forever. We all make mistakes, but making them, even big ones, does not constitute failure. If we admit to failing yesterday, we are also making a statement that we're wiser today. We place a premium on people who are wise.

How does one gain wisdom? Usually by making errors and learning from them. So often my insight has come as a sudden flashback from the past, when, in the midst of some situation, I suddenly remembered the pain and lessons I learned from similar incidents in my life.

The greatest mistake people make is to stop stepping out and taking chances. We can't walk around with our heads down forever. We must choose to see mistakes for what they are—just part of being human. We can choose to learn from them and go on.

Corrie Ten Boom said it best: "God can give a straight blow with a crooked stick. He blesses us in spite of our blunders."

Some trials are a result of our dumb doings and sinful acts. As humans, sometimes we do stupid things and pay a dear price as a result. Such trials are some of the hardest to swallow and deal with. Believe me, I know, and so does King David, Samson, Abraham, and even Peter. But go we must and trust God to redeem even the trials that we bring upon ourselves.

It's worth noting that AC today often puts more emphasis upon sin than it does on our Savior. We have what I call a sin-complex, that is, we love talking about how the choir leader got caught up with the organ player in a tumultuous affair. We sometimes seem to get a spiritual high by rehearsing all the details of the ordeal, and eagerly telling all our spiritual cronies about the shocking news.

We need to change the way we think.

A NEW PERSPECTIVE

I might be misunderstood in what I'm about to say, but I think there are times when falling into sin is the only thing that will get a person serious about letting God change who he is.

There are people who sometimes live with sin in their hearts for so long that they become immune to its presence. They somehow convince themselves that it's quite normal for their sin to be there. But once they act upon it and make reality out of their fantasy, they suffer a much needed wake-up call. As a result, they invite God into some of the deep recesses of their heart that He's never been allowed into before. They become willing to submit themselves to godly counsel, and become so broken that they are ashamed to even entertain the sinful thoughts they were so immune to living with for so many years. In other words, their falling into sin actually works out for their good.

When we put this in the overall perspective of God's plan for an individual's life, we see that because of the person's sin, he will grow to be a much more productive believer than he would have ever been had the disgraceful act never occurred. He will become a better Christian, spouse, and parent. Most of all, he will never allow that sin any place in his life again. He could have wasted decades by letting the inward sin sap all his productive energy.

In no way am I condoning or encouraging sinful living. We all know that every time an overt act of sin is rebelliously acted out in our lives, something dies inwardly, and we pay a high price for that awful deed. It is by far much better to not expose our families and ourselves to the horrible pain sin causes.

Sometimes we leave God no choice as to how He can affect a deep change in our lives. And this is where Romans 8:28 can become a powerful tool in the hands of an all-loving and forgiving God: "And we know that God causes all things to work together for good to those who love God, to those who are called according to *His* purpose."

FORGIVENESS TRUMPS FAILURE

My prayer is twofold here. First, I pray that we will let God deal with the sins of our hearts, so we won't have to let sin have its way in our lives. By this, we avoid the overt sin that reveals the part of our heart that is wicked in God's sight. For it was Jesus who declared, "You have heard that it was said, *'You shall not commit adultery';* but I say to you that everyone who looks at a woman with lust for her has already committed adultery with her in his heart" (Matthew 5:27-28).

Whatever we think about long enough in our hearts works its way into some kind of outward behavior over time. Most sins of the heart don't stay there forever.

67

Second, I pray that when we see people fall into sin and confess it, we immediately make a commitment to not talk about the trespass but instead to rejoice in the fact that we have a loving Savior who forgives.

How refreshing it would be to have someone, upon hearing that a brother or sister had fallen into a terrible sin, respond by saying, "Can we just stop for a moment and thank God for sending His Son Jesus Christ to die on the cross for our sins?"

We should rejoice more about having a Savior than we should about having a sin issue. Certainly, sin is horrible, but the fact that we have a Savior is more important. It is the very essence of the heart of the gospel message.

We don't want to lighten or lessen the seriousness of sin, but in the same token, we most certainly don't want to make it bigger than the awesome love of our Savior and the incredible act of love He showed when He hung on the cross. We must never view our own problems or the problems that others go through without seeing them from the perspective of the cross.

Adversities are not the biggest issues in our lives, but the way we respond to them is what defeats us.

Five

THE KIND OF PRAYER THAT WORKS

Before we can pray, "Lord, Thy Kingdom come,"
we must be willing to pray, "My Kingdom go."
— ALAN REDPATH

Sad but true, there have been studies done down through the years that show most Christians don't pray over an average of three minutes a day. Why, you may ask? Because they don't believe in prayer. It's that simple.

Oh, they say they believe in prayer, but they really don't. To *say* we believe in something and to *show* that we believe in something are two entirely different things. Words are cheap. I believe that the lack of praying people in this country is a clear indication that we don't understand the rewards of prayer, nor do we know how to pray.

I believe that when the people of God are shown how to pray, and they are shown that prayer truly does work, they will begin to pray a lot. Let's turn to the Bible to see what it says about this topic.

First, the Bible teaches us that prayer is effective:

- Genesis 20:17: "Abraham prayed to God, and God healed Abimelech and his wife and his maids, so that they bore children."
- Genesis 25:21: "Isaac prayed to the Lord on behalf of his wife, because she was barren; and the Lord answered him

and Rebekah his wife conceived."
• Numbers 11:2: "The people therefore cried out to Moses, and Moses prayed to the Lord and the fire died out."
• 1 Samuel 1:27: "For this boy I prayed, and the Lord has given me my petition which I asked of Him."

I could go on and on with more examples, but I think you get the point: God answers prayer. Calling on God worked for the people in the Bible, and it will work for you and me once we learn how to open the doors of heaven.

Pay attention to what Jesus said in these following verses. I've italicized some words and phrases so that prayer will start to make more sense to you.

• John 14:13: *"Whatever* you ask in *My name,* that *will I do,* so that the Father may be glorified in the Son."
• John 14:14: "If you ask Me *anything* in *My name, I will do it."*
• John 15:7: *"If you abide in Me,* and My *words (rhemas) abide in you,* ask *whatever* you wish, and it *will be done for you."*
• John 15:16: "You did not choose Me but I chose you, and appointed you that you would go and bear fruit, and that your fruit would remain, so that *whatever* you ask of the Father in *My name* He may *give to you."*
• John 16:23: "In that day you will not question Me about anything. Truly, truly, I say to you, if you ask the Father for *anything in My name,* He will *give it to you."*

The first thing I want you to remember is that we have to ask in His name. This simply means that we are to ask what Jesus would if He were standing right here with us. This is where it gets tricky, and most Christians miss it. If you can grasp this, then you will have many more prayers answered in your life. In simple

70

terms, Jesus asked the Father for anything and everything He needed in order for God's will to be done. If God had an assignment for Jesus, then Jesus expected the Father to give Him whatever He needed to complete the task.

We can expect the same, once we qualify the tasks God has for us. Below are some assignments I believe God has given to all believers:

1. Raise a godly family.
2. Serve God by using our spiritual gifts.
3. Stand above sin and live a righteous life.
4. Provide a living for our families.

Number one, I believe it is God's will for my life and yours that we raise godly families. Whatever we need to accomplish this assignment will be given to us if we ask for it in prayer. Let me illustrate what I mean. I taught both my children to hear God's voice because I felt that it was pertinent for each and every believer to learn to hear from God. The theme behind my book *Conspiracy of Silence* is that if we don't learn to hear God's voice, we are going to suffer and lose many things that we were never meant to lose, such as our marriages, health, kids, and ministries. Learning to walk close to God and hear His voice is mandatory to a life pleasing to God.

"DAD, COME HERE"

One day, I walked into my daughter Tara's bedroom, and she was very upset over something. She was about sixteen years old at the time. I remember comforting and telling her God had promised He wouldn't let any temptation come into her life that she couldn't handle; that He had promised to make a way of escape for her each and every time a temptation presented itself. Then I said, "Tara, you're old enough now to start hearing God's voice for yourself.

Ask Him to confirm what I've just told you, and He will."

It wasn't more than ten minutes later when Tara opened her bedroom door and cried out, "Dad, come here." She was crying and through broken words I heard her say, "Look at what I turned to in my Bible after praying and asking God to speak to me."

She handed me her Bible that was opened to 1 Corinthians 10, and she pointed to verse 13. It read, "No temptation has overtaken you but such as is common to man; and God is faithful, who will not allow you to be tempted beyond what you are able, but with the temptation will provide the way of escape also, so that you may be able to endure it." God divinely spoke to her.

The point I want you to see is that I could ask God to do this with complete confidence and faith, and be assured that He would because it was part of His divine plan for me to raise godly kids. It's what I asked in His name.

A Lesson for Josh

There's a similar story I can relate concerning our son Joshua. When he was around fifteen years old, I sat with him on the living room couch and I shared my heart. "Josh, God's told me that He wants to start speaking to you. He wants to develop a more personal one-on-one relationship. So here's what we are going to do. On this piece of paper I'm going to write the name of a person God has laid upon my heart. I'm not going to show you who it is, and then I am going to ask God to reveal that same name to you. I guarantee He will absolutely do that, just watch and see."

So I prayed, "Oh God, please reveal to Josh the name that You have put on my heart and the name I've written on this piece of paper. In Jesus' name I thank You for doing this. Amen."

Keep in mind that at the time we probably had about three thousand people attending our church. Josh just sat there for a few minutes and then he said, "Tom Touchstone is the only person that comes to my mind."

"Josh," I exclaimed, "look at the name I've written down on this paper. It's Tom Touchstone. You can hear God, Josh. Isn't it wonderful?"

Hearing God's voice is part of the heavenly assignment He has given to us. It's a prayer you can pray in Jesus' name.

KEEP ON ASKING

There's something about prayer that many people don't understand. Some prayers are only answered after a season of prayer. Not all our prayers are answered right away. Jesus tells us this in Luke 11:5-10:

> Then [Jesus] said to them, "Suppose one of you has a friend, and goes to him at midnight and says to him, 'Friend, lend me three loaves; for a friend of mine has come to me from a journey, and I have nothing to set before him'; and from inside he answers and says, 'Do not bother me; the door has already been shut and my children and I are in bed; I cannot get up and give you anything.'
>
> "I'll tell you even though he will not get up and give him anything because he is his friend, yet because of his persistence he will get up and give him as much as he needs.
>
> "So I say to you, ask, and it will be given to you; seek and you will find; knock and it will be opened. For everyone who asks, receives; and he who seeks, finds; and to him who knocks, it will be opened."

The Greek word for *ask* in verse nine is in the present imperative, which means that it's something to be done in the future that involves continuous and repeated action. In other words, if we ask and keep on asking it will be given to us.

73

James said basically the same thing when he wrote about healing prayer in James 5:13-18:

> *Is anyone among you suffering? Then he must pray. Is anyone cheerful? He is to sing praises. Is anyone among you sick? Then he must call the elders of the church and they are to pray over him, anointing him with oil in the name of the Lord; and the prayer offered in faith will restore the one who is sick, and the Lord will raise him up, and if he has committed sins, they will be forgiven him.*
>
> *Therefore, confess your sins to one another, and pray for one another so that you may be healed. The <u>effective</u> prayer of a righteous man can accomplish much.*
>
> *Elijah was a man with a nature like ours, and he prayed earnestly that it might not rain, and it did not rain on the earth for three years and six months. Then he prayed again, and the sky poured rain and the earth produced its fruit.*

The Greek word for "effective" is *energeo,* which means "active, energetic, persistent, and ongoing." There are some instances when we can't pray just once and expect results. In fact, a general rule is to pray and continue to pray until we either receive an answer, or God instructs us to stop praying.

There's an interesting story in 1 Kings 18 that illustrates this. Elijah had just prophesied to King Ahab that, after a season of drought in the land, it was going to rain. And Elijah traveled up to Mount Carmel and prayed for rain. We can read the account in 1 Kings 18:41-46:

> *Now Elijah said to Ahab, "Go up, eat and drink; for there is the sound of the roar of a heavy shower. So Ahab went up to eat and drink. But Elijah went up to the top of Carmel; and he crouched down on the earth and put his*

face between his knees. And he said to his servant, "Go up now, look toward the sea." So he went up and looked and said, "There is nothing." And he said, "Go back" seven times.

It came about at the seventh time, that he said, "Behold, a cloud as small as a man's hand is coming up from the sea." And he said, "Go up, say to Ahab, 'Prepare your chariot and go down, so that the heavy shower does not stop you."

In a little while the sky grew black with clouds and wind, and there was a heavy shower. And Ahab rode and went to Jezreel.

Then the hand of the Lord was on Elijah, and he girded up his loins and outran Ahab to Jezreel.

Notice Elijah's attitude when he prays. It doesn't matter to him if he prays two times or two hundred times. He's not going to stop praying until it rains. God has given him a promise and he's going to pray that promise into a manifestation. He, as I often say, has thrown his hat over the fence. He keeps asking his servant to go and look toward the sea to see if any rain clouds are forming. He seems to be very confident that sooner or later they will appear, and he's not embarrassed to let everyone see his faith. It can't be any other way because God is faithful to His Word.

One time—go look! Two times—go look! Three times— go look! Four times—go look! I have to wonder that if it had been you or me praying, would we have thrown in the towel after the third time, or maybe even the first time, when nothing happened?

EFFECTIVE PRAYER

I love what Jesus said in Matthew 11:12: "From the days of John the Baptist until now the kingdom of heaven suffers violence and violent men take it by force."

75

I picture Elijah as a warrior wearing war paint and violently praying for God's will to be done. Nothing could stand in his way of making the will of God become a manifested reality. He was a man on a mission, not like some Christians when they pray their polite, politically correct prayers. This man meant business!

James used this story about Elijah to illustrate how healing prayer works. It's the effective prayer of a righteous man that can accomplish much.

In my book *Conspiracy of Silence,* I tell how my doctor at UCLA Medical Center only gave me four to five years to live, but how, through fervent, effective prayer, God saved me from the death sentence I was given. I had to pray every day for over two years before I saw any manifestation of healing.

THE RIGHT NAME

Back in 1980, my wife Debbie became pregnant with our second child. In those days, ultrasounds were not common, so we didn't have any way of knowing if we were expecting a boy or a girl. Now, because I already had a beautiful daughter, I really wanted a son, so I started praying. When Debbie was near the end of her pregnancy, she asked the doctor to give us his educated guess of whether we were having a boy or a girl. By measuring the heartbeat, he guessed a little girl. But I had been praying every day. We had to choose a name, and we had always agreed that if we had a boy, we would like to name him Joshua. But we wanted God to help us pick out the right name.

One day, Debbie, Tara, and I were driving over to Lancaster to visit my father-in-law, who was in the hospital, and we began to talk about what we were going to name our baby. Debbie said she really felt like it was going to be a boy, and we were to name him Joshua. Later on, when we arrived and entered the hospital, we resumed the conversation. Just as we were going through a door in the hospital corridor I asked Debbie, "Are you sure God said to name him Joshua?"

As I asked her that question, I looked at the door I was about to enter and had my hand on. It was labeled "The Joshua Room." We both looked at each other and laughed. Could this be a confirmation of what we were feeling?

Well, we don't live our lives in such a fashion where everything is definitely God; some things just might be coincidence. I've seen some Christians who are so mystical and "spiritual" that they scare me.

Later that month we drove to the coast for a mini-vacation, and, as usual, we went to the beach to get some sun rays. When we found a good place to lay out, I knelt down and began to dig a hole for Debbie's tummy to fit in, so she could get some sun on her back. (By the way, Debbie is only 4'11" tall and weighs a whopping 94 pounds.) As I dug, there were what looked like two servicemen sitting in lawn chairs about 10 feet away. One of them looked up at me and stated the obvious. *"You* guys are going to have a baby, huh?"

I said, "Yep, in just a few weeks."

To which one of them replied, "A boy or a girl?"

"I hope a boy," I answered.

"Do you have a name picked out?" one of them asked.

"Nah, not really," I said.

"You ought to consider the name Joshua," he announced to my astonishment.

There it was again, possibly the second confirmation.

You never know when the Lord is using you to be a confirmation for someone else who is seeking God. These servicemen will never even remember this incident, let alone realize that God used them on that hot, summer day.

We must always stay prayed up and filled with the Holy Spirit. We might not even be aware until we get to heaven just how many times God used us on earth. This is why I so much believe in doing the things that come strongly to mind, even if they seem to make no sense at the time, especially when we are filled with the Holy Spirit.

Now, I began to wonder if God wasn't trying to confirm the fact that we were supposed to name the baby Joshua. It never entered our minds, at this point, that it could be a little girl. Every time I prayed, the idea of naming our baby Joshua grew stronger and stronger.

Is it God Talking?

I've often told people that one of many ways we can determine whether God is saying something or not, is by taking the issue before Him in prayer for ten days. And while in prayer, if what we're praying for is God's will, then our spirit will grow stronger in the process. And if it's not God's will, our spirit will be very uneasy.

For example, the Apostle Paul asked the Lord to take the thorn in his flesh away from him. He probably prayed strongly the first time, with a lot of conviction. And the second time he likely had less conviction, and the third time he perhaps had to struggle to even bring it up in prayer.

On the other hand, when Elijah prayed the first time for rain, he no doubt had a great deal of conviction and fire in his words. The second time, he probably had as much strong belief and enthusiasm as the first. The third time the intensity was staying the same, if not getting stronger. The same with the fourth, fifth, sixth, and the seventh times.

I've found the ten-day method to be a very reliable test to add to other confirmations when trying to find out if something is God's will or not. Remember, don't just take one factor by itself, but see all these things as just a part of His big equation.

"OKAY GOD, I GET IT"

Every time I prayed over what to name our child, the name Joshua sprang to mind, along with a strong sense of conviction that this was the name God had picked out for our baby.

Well, the final confirmation came the night that Debbie was in labor at the hospital. I was trying to coach her through the labor with all the infinite knowledge and wisdom I had learned in our Lamaze courses. Meanwhile, this guy in the television movie that was being shown in our room, kept yelling out, "Where's my son Joshua? Joshua! Joshua! Joshua!"

Finally I looked up at the ceiling of the hospital room and said, "Okay God, I get it; his name shall be Joshua."

Well, you guessed it; we welcomed a healthy seven-pound boy, and we called him Joshua. Now in the Hebrew his name is *Yehoshua,* and it means "the Lord is my salvation." Some dictionaries define its meaning as "a deliverer of God's people."

PRAYING AND SMILING

Throughout Joshua's childhood, I kept in mind that God named him and obviously had a great purpose for his life. Up until Joshua's senior year in high school, I knew he loved God, but he didn't show it a lot in his lifestyle. I mean he went to church, didn't do drugs, nor did he drink. Occasionally I'd see him reading his Bible. Overall, he was just a good, average American Christian kid. But, at the time, he wasn't what I would have called a deliverer of God's people in the making!

Josh knew I wanted him to go into the ministry, and so, as he made preparations about what college he would attend after high school, he would often say to me, "Dad, I know you want me to go into the ministry, but that's not the direction I'm going with my life."

I would smile, nod my head, and say something like, "I know, son."

But weekly I prayed that God would override Josh's wishes and cause His perfect will to be done in his young life.

Over and over again Joshua would remind me, "Dad, I'm not going into the ministry." But I kept praying and smiling.

Soon his tune began to change a little, "Dad, if I were to go into the ministry, how would I go about it?"

I kept smiling and praying. At the same time, I saw a fire of love for God begin to burn in Josh, and I knew that the Lord's will would be done.

Before long he was asking, "Dad, what do I need to do to go into the ministry?"

Today, Josh is one of our main teaching pastors and is a big influence in the direction the church is going.

A COVERING FOR OUR FAMILIES

Parents don't seem to recognize the great responsibility they have in raising godly families. Children are like small, fresh balls of clay. If put into the hands of a skilled artisan, the outcome can be totally awesome. But if put into the hands of a lazy couch potato, the results are pathetically sad.

Maybe you've heard it said, "Big mean people make little mean people, and lazy big people make lazy little people, and big people of character make little people of character."

As parents, we have to wake up to the realization of the powerful role prayer plays in raising godly kids. It's my fear that many, if not most, Christians fail to see the disastrous results of a lack of prayer. When we fail to cover our families with prayer, the enemy busily plants seeds of discord, rebellion, and worldliness in them.

As a parent, it is my responsibility to overcome the spirit the world is trying to instill in my kids. And I do so by daily praying a spiritual covering over them. The Bible says we have not because we ask not. Are we continually asking God to surround our kids with His physical as well as spiritual protection? Are we praying for good friends to come into their lives? Are we calling on God that they will develop a hunger for the Lord? Or, are we praying for them at all?

A PRAYER THAT WOULD NOT DIE

Believe me, young children do not turn into spiritual giants by just throwing them out into the world with a wing and a prayer. I believe that as Christian parents, if we know how to pray, we can even influence our child's decision in picking a lifelong mate.

When Josh was about sixteen years of age, I started praying concerning who he would someday marry. I kept visualizing a picture of a sandy, blonde-haired young lady in my mind. I saw the image so clearly that I felt sure that if I ever saw her I would recognize her.

Well, about five years later I was speaking in chapel at the Christian high school at our church, and I saw who appeared to be the young lady I'd envisioned when I prayed years earlier. Something triggered the thought, "This is Josh's wife-to-be."

At the time, it didn't make a lot of sense because this young lady was only a freshman in high school and Joshua had already graduated. Too much of an age difference, possibly? I mean Josh already had a girlfriend, and I couldn't see him waiting around for this young girl to grow up. But nevertheless, something in my heart told me she was the one.

When I shared this with my wife, she curiously came down to the church to see who I was talking about. Immediately, she felt the same way I did. We found out the girl's name was Ashley. So we began to pray every day, "Oh, God, put the desire in Ashley's heart for Josh, and put a desire in Josh's heart for Ashley."

The more we prayed that first year, the more it looked like it would never happen. But we kept praying. It wasn't long before Ashley found another boyfriend, and it seemed as though Joshua was getting very serious with another girl. But this turn of events didn't stop us from praying daily, week after week, month after month.

When you are calling on God for His will in your life, you will know whether you should keep praying. It will be undeniable. As I said earlier, your faith will remain strong, and you will feel anointed to keep the matter before God. Furthermore, God will consistently and yet sporadically give you little signs to let you know you're on track so that you won't grow weary and give up.

If God had a call upon Joshua's life, then I figured it was more important to Him than it was to Debbie and me that he marry the right person. I guess you could say that God was partnering with us in our prayers. It was like the Lord kept telling us not to be discouraged but keep praying.

A DIVINE BREAKTHROUGH

Jesus told Peter, as recorded in Matthew 16:19, "I will give you the keys of the kingdom of heaven; and whatever you bind on earth shall have been bound in heaven, and whatever you loose on earth, shall have been loosed in heaven."

A lot of Christians don't understand that if we fail to pray, God won't just make some things happen. He has made us His body on the earth, and it's up to us to do as the original humans, Adam and Eve did—go forth and subdue the world around them.

We have been equipped to do the Lord's bidding on this planet, to enforce God's will in situations in which we have authority, and to do this through prayer and spiritual warfare.

Every time I'd become discouraged in praying for Josh and Ashley to fall in love and some day get married, God would do something to encourage me and get me back to praying. Debbie didn't get disheartened as much as I did. She knew that she knew that she knew God would answer our prayers. Continually, over the four years we prayed, Debbie would say to me, "Ron, did you pray for Josh and Ashley today?"

Three years went by and nothing changed, although Ashley worked in the same office as Josh as a church college intern. It seemed as though they barely knew each other existed. At one time, when Josh was Ashley's immediate supervisor, I'd occasionally see them interact with one another. But it was so cold, calculated, and always so businesslike. The more I watched them around one another, the more my mind told me, "There is absolutely no way this will ever come about." To me, it seemed like they wanted nothing to do with each other.

As I look back, it was probably just a sign of good character. After all, they each had a different boyfriend and girlfriend, and both seemed to be true and loyal to the people they were dating. In hindsight, it was an admirable thing.

Don't Lose Heart

One day Debbie and I were vacationing in San Luis Obispo and we were getting a little weary over the Josh and Ashley thing. This time it was both of us who were disheartened. We had been praying so long and nothing was moving forward.

We were at a Christian bookstore in San Luis Obispo, and while browsing through some books, I came upon one particular volume that grabbed my attention. Written on one page was, "Don't get discouraged. Once God puts a desire in your soul for something He will give it to you, if you only keep praying and don't lose heart."

Bingo! I felt this was definitely a word for Debbie and me, so I went to look for my wife in the bookstore, so I could show her what I had read. I found her, but before I could open my mouth, she said, "Ron, I believe God has just spoken to me through this book I have here." And she went on to tell me how this Christian writer had gone through a situation with her child very similar to what we were going through. The author wrote that she believed when your son or daughter finds the right person he or she was supposed to marry; the whole family would know it. There would be no doubts at all.

Debbie compared this author's statement to how we felt strongly that Josh was supposed to marry Ashley. Although he had dated several very nice young Christian women, we just never felt any of them was the girl that God had chosen for Josh.

Both of us stood there with books in our hands that we believed God had brought to our attention to encourage us not to stop praying. And to top it all off, when we left the bookstore and went across the street to a salad bar to grab a bite to eat, a young waitress approached our table with a large, friendly smile and said, "Hi, my name is Ashley. I'll be your waitress today. If I can help you with anything, let me know."

We both looked at each other and laughed. God was going out of His way to let us know that we were smack dab in the center of His will. And we had many more occasions like this. There was also that old true standby confirmation that every time we prayed, the conviction that Ashley was the one grew stronger and stronger.

OFF TO LAS VEGAS

One day, after we had been praying for over three and half years without seeing any results at all, I was walking through the church office, and I spoke to Ashley. She seemed to be down and not her usual self, so I asked her if she wanted to talk and she did. She shared with me that she had just broken up with her boyfriend, and she felt a little downhearted. I tried my best to be of encouragement, and I prayed for her.

That day I went home and told Debbie. Now Debbie and Ashley had already developed a relationship, so they were kind of close. At that time, I was pastoring two churches, one in Bakersfield, California and the other in Las Vegas, Nevada. Well it was my week to be in Las Vegas, and Debbie had this great idea to invite Ashley to go with us for the week.

So, Debbie invited Ashley to join us, and she gladly accepted our invitation.

I forgot to add that Joshua was also in the process of breaking up with his girlfriend at the time. He just didn't feel that the relationship was right for him.

I normally conducted the Thursday-night Bible study myself, but on this particular Thursday, I asked one of the elders in our California church to speak in Vegas. His name was Charlie Garcia. (Now, I don't have time to go into the story of this man, who is now at home in heaven with Jesus, but it's sufficient to say that he was one of the most godly men I've ever met and probably will ever meet.) Charlie agreed to speak for me in Vegas, but I was still committed to be there with him that Thursday evening.

Debbie and I went home to pack, so we could pick Ashley up and head out. When we got to the house, Josh was there, so I decided to ask him if he would like to go to Vegas with us and get away for a few days. He inquired if anyone was going with us, probably because occasionally we had friends accompany us.

I casually replied, "Mom, Ashley, and I are going."

He quickly retorted, "Dad, don't go there. I won't go unless God tells me to go."

And we left it at that.

THE REST IS HISTORY

What happened next blew me away. Not more than three hours passed when Charlie Garcia called and told me that he had a dream about him speaking in Vegas the night before, and he saw Josh in the audience. He said he really felt like Josh was supposed to be there for reasons he did not know. He thought perhaps he'd need Josh to help him illustrate a point. He asked if our son could somehow go to Vegas in case he needed him.

I passed Charlie's request on to Josh, so he decided to make the trip. We needed to take two cars, for business reasons, so I drove one car, and Josh went with me. Debbie and Ashley traveled in the other vehicle.

When we arrived in Vegas, Debbie and I had to call some parishioners, so I told Josh and Ashley they could take one of the cars and go down to the Strip or wherever, if they wanted to.

Josh looked at Ashley and asked, "Do you want to go?"

She replied, "I guess, if you do."

The rest is history, or what I call "His-story."

At the writing of this book, they are now married and doing fantastic. Is God totally awesome or what? It took almost four years of constant, consistent prayer, but it paid off. Josh and Ashley chose to get married, and now I can't wait to see what God has in store for their lives.

AUTHORITY AND AGREEMENT

I just wonder how the future of those who read this book will be transformed as they learn of the power they possess with prayer. The majority of Christians don't realize that when they pray in Jesus' name they will have results.

I become frustrated when Christian parents tell me that they don't feel good about the girl or boy their child is dating, and yet they don't realize that God has equipped them with the necessary tool—namely prayer—to take authority over the situation and bring it into agreement with God's will. God did not leave us defenseless on this earth to become nothing more than people of random happenstance. He has called us to be men and women of authority who clearly see our calling to make sure that God's will is accomplished in the areas of life we are responsible for. As I said at the beginning of this chapter, to pray in the name of Jesus is to pray the way He would if He were us.

THE FATHER'S WILL

Jesus understood His role on this earth. He told His disciples, "My food is to do the will of Him who sent Me and to accomplish His work" (John 4:34). He knew He was called to do the Father's will, and in the process, He would use prayer as a tool to obtain all the provisions He needed.

Jesus could pray with confidence once He knew the Father's will, and so can we. We can know the desire of God, first by knowing the Word of God, because scripture makes clear to us the revealed will of God.

For example:

- It is God's will to save anyone who calls upon the name of the Lord.
- It is God's will to forgive us of our sins.
- It is God's will to hear our prayers.
- It is God's will to give us wisdom.
- It is God's will to fill us with the Holy Spirit.
- It is God's will to supply our needs.
- It is God's will to give us strength over sin.
- It is God's will to work all things out for our good.
- It is God's will to reveal to us our spiritual gift.

The list is long. Study the Word, and discover these truths for yourself. Yet I've met Christians who can't name more than one thing that they positively know to be God's will for their lives.

No wonder there is so little prayer in the average church. We don't know what to pray for—or even how to pray.

It's important for us to understand that the will of God for us doesn't always happen automatically. More often than not, it has to be prayed into being. God basically says, "Here's the stuff I want to give you. All these things are My will for you. But you must bring them into existence and manifestation through prayer."

It is prayer that makes His will a reality. Jesus illustrates this by what He told His disciples in Luke 10:2: "The harvest is plentiful, but the laborers are few; therefore beseech the Lord of the harvest to send out laborers into His harvest."

Pay attention to the word *beseech*. It basically means, "I beg you to beg me." In other words, Jesus lets us know that God won't accomplish His will automatically without the people of God activating this through prayer. It is vital for us to grasp this.

KEYS TO THE KINGDOM

God has left us on this earth well equipped with the Holy Spirit, the power of prayer, the Spirit of authority, angels at our disposal, and wisdom at our fingertips. He has left us with these keys to the kingdom, so that we can accomplish His will on earth—not for fulfilling our will, but *His*.

Regarding the Spirit of authority, again this is a tool God has given us that very few Christians know anything about. If we studied scripture, we would quickly see that the New Testament church was much more informed about how to walk with God than we are. They spent at least three periods of time in prayer daily. They prayed in the morning, in the afternoon, and in the evening. Now these sessions of communicating with God kept them filled with the Holy Spirit and the knowledge of the Father's will, so that when they went out into the marketplace, they were able to walk in authority.

Let's read what happened in Acts 3:1-9:

> *Now Peter and John were going up to the temple at the ninth hour, the hour of prayer. And a man who had been lame from his mother's womb was being carried along, whom they used to set down every day at the gate of the temple which is called Beautiful, in order to beg alms of those who were entering the temple. When he saw Peter*

and John about to go into the temple, he began asking to receive alms.

But Peter, along with John, fixed his gaze on him and said, "Look at us!"

And he began to give them his attention, expecting to receive something from them.

But Peter said, "I do not possess silver and gold, but what I do have I give to you: In the name of Jesus Christ the Nazarene—walk!" And seizing him by the right hand, he raised him up; and immediately his feet and his ankles were strengthened. And with a leap, he stood upright and began to walk; and he entered the temple with them, walking and leaping and praising God.

Notice that when Peter and John saw this man in need, they didn't stop and pray, "Oh, Lord, help me, help me, help me." But they spoke God's will into existence: "Silver and gold have I none, but what I *do have* I give to you: *In the name of Jesus Christ, the Nazarene— walk!"*

Now this is not just an isolated case. It was a way of life for the New Testament church, and they are our models for Christian living. This is why we are told that in the early church there was always a sense of awe. In other words, when they got together, one person would testify, "Guess what God did in my life today?" And after he shared his story, they would be amazed. This happened so often that the Bible says there was a "Spirit of awe" in the New Testament church. Where has such a Spirit gone in the church today?

They were continually devoting themselves to the apostles' teaching and to fellowship, to the breaking of bread and to prayer. Everyone kept feeling a sense of awe; and many wonders and signs were taking place through the apostles. And all those who had believed were together and had all things in common; and they began selling their property and possessions and were sharing them with all, as anyone might have need. Day by day continuing with one mind in the temple, and breaking bread from house to house, they were taking their meals together with gladness and sincerity of heart, praising God, and having favor with all the people. And the Lord was adding to their number day by day those who were being saved (Acts 2:42-47).

Again, this wasn't just a rare example. Read Acts 5:1-10, Acts 13:9-11, Acts 14:8-10, Acts 16-18, and Acts 20:9-12. Some may argue, but the apostles had a different calling than we do. We are not New Testament apostles. But Paul wasn't one of the original twelve, nor was Phillip the evangelist, who had miracles happen in his life. Barnabas and Silas weren't apostles. Neither was Elisha or Gideon.

It was said of both Daniel and Joseph that the Spirit of the divine God lived in them, and they weren't apostles. They could, however, interpret dreams and obviously had supernatural gifts working in them.

WHAT'S THE DRIVING FORCE?

I don't know why some of us insist that the supernatural lifestyle existed only for a short time, while the Bible was being written, and after that, including today, God has ordained for us the "age of spiritual boredom." We're supposed to fold our hands and be nice until the Lord comes back for us, and *then* we can once again live a very adventuresome, challenging, Spirit-filled lifestyle. It makes absolutely no sense. And then, to top off this ludicrous idea, is the fact that absolutely nowhere in the Bible does it even hint that God wants us to view life this way. There aren't any scriptures to back up the ultra-conservative Christians who teach this.

Please don't get me wrong, I'm not saying that all of us should go around raising the dead and opening blind eyes, because not everyone in the Bible did those things. I'm just telling you that we should live in such a way that bears witness with the reality that God's Spirit is the driving force of our lives. We should hear God speak to us daily and sense His presence every waking hour. We should see angels and demons working in and around us and be open to spiritual dreams and revelations as well as to visions and prophetic words.

It is truly one exciting journey to walk with God just the way the people in the Bible did. I find it hard to understand why any theologian or pastor would want to force upon us a belief system that says God now lives in a box. And He can't allow Himself to speak anymore to mortal humans because He no longer wants to personally interact with them.

If you ask one of these Christians why God doesn't work today as He did in Bible times, their best reply is: "He has His reasons."

Excuse me, but that's absolutely ridiculous. One of the main reasons why I feel so many believers are backsliding is because they are bored sitting in their pews. Nothing they are learning is challenging their spirit. We hear it all the time: "Church is boring and has nothing to offer me."

But if people started learning how to hear God's voice, and about demons, angels, visions, revelations, how to have your prayers answered, how to invoke God's presence, what to expect when we get to heaven, how to use our spiritual weapons, how to find our spiritual gifts, how the hundred-fold blessing works, how to confuse the enemy, and how to bind up and loosen things on the earth, then men and women would be excited to enter God's house.

YOUR DIVINE ASSIGNMENT

I find it so interesting that in many recent surveys people have ememberNo

said that they couldn't identify with the modern day church and that they think it's dull and lifeless, but they do consider Jesus to be a cool person and find Him interesting. What does this say about us, the body of Christ?

We know that Jesus never lied, not even once, in His entire life. Read what He said in John 14:12: "Truly, truly I say to you, he who believes in Me, the works that I do, he will do also; and greater works than these he will do; because I go to the Father."

How do we respond to a passage like this? How do our ultraconservative Bible teachers explain away such verses? They must work awfully hard. I'm so glad I don't have to sit up nights to think of a way to make the Word of God fit into my belief system.

Look at the way Jesus interacted in the marketplace. We know He spent a great amount of time on the mountain praying, but among the people He used His spiritual authority to speak things into existence. For example, He was always using words such as, "Be healed," "Spirit be gone," "Wind be still," "Lazarus come forth," "Get thee behind Me Satan," "Rise and walk," and "Let it be to you according to your faith."

In addition, He cursed the fig tree, commanded fevers to leave, and told men what they were thinking. Read the Bible for yourself. Again, He was God's Son, and He was a master at what He did.

We shouldn't be discouraged because we can't perform the miracles He did, but we can grow toward that end and can start activating our spiritual giftings in small ways. This is how we will mature as Christians.

I have been living this life of faith for over thirty years, and with God's help, have taught thousands of others to live it also. It's absolutely the only Christian lifestyle I have ever known or ever want to know. I can't even think about trading places with the monotonous, ineffective, unbiblical style of believing being taught in some churches today.

COMPLETE THE TASK!

All things are possible through prayer. We know that one of our divine assignments is to raise a godly family. Anything we need to accomplish, we can pray for in Jesus' name and have the confidence that God will answer. The Apostle Paul wrote, "And my God *will* supply all your needs according to His riches in glory in Christ Jesus" (Philippians 4:19).

Another one of our assignments is to serve God by using our spiritual gifts. When I was diagnosed with leukemia, I went to the Lord and asked if my time of service on earth was over. I waited for a few weeks before I received an answer to that prayer. Once He made known to me that my work here was not complete, I then set out to conquer my cancer through prayer. I knew I'd be victorious because I was on a divine assignment. I felt much like the Apostle Paul did in Philippians 1:21-25:

> *For to me, to live is Christ and to die is gain. But if I am to live on in the flesh, this will mean fruitful labor for me; and I do not know which to choose. But I am hard-pressed from both directions, having the desire to depart and be with Christ, for that is very much better; yet to remain on in the flesh is more necessary for your sake. Convinced of this, I know that I will remain and continue with you all for your progress and joy in the faith...*

I knew my purpose. I knew I had to pray until I received a manifestation of healing. (Again, you can read a more thorough account about this in my book *Conspiracy of Silence.*) So anything I needed to complete this task, I also obtained through prayer (things such as resources for buildings, vehicles, etc.).

Discover it for Yourself

Do you know why we hear about so many missionary miracles? It's because they are on divine assignment. If they need to get to a certain location because they must minister there, God will make a way. And this is also true for us.

Some of the amazing God-stories of missionaries now make a lot of sense to me. I once read about one man, who needed to be in a certain location to preach, but fog had set in on the coastland and the boat he was going to take couldn't leave port. So he informed the captain that he would just have to pray the fog away. And praise God, he did! There are many more stories like this in the biographies of our Christian forefathers.

My purpose in writing this book is to inspire you to start searching out the Word for yourself. I want you to feel an obligation to personally discover if what I am teaching you is good Bible doctrine or not. Let me remind you of what Jesus said in John chapter 7:17: "If anyone is willing to do His will, he will know of the teaching whether it is of God, or whether I speak from Myself."

Then in John 5:31-32 Jesus declares, "If I alone testify about Myself, My testimony is not true. There is another who testifies of Me, and I know that the testimony which He gives about Me is true."

I truly believe one of my divine assignments is *to stand above sin and live a righteous life.* This simply means that I can pray for whatever I need in order to complete my assignment.

A Concerned Mom

A pastor once told the story of how a traveling woman evangelist, who preached at his church, mentioned that whenever she prayed for a husband she used to hang a pair of pants on one of her bedposts. And at night she'd pray, "Dear God, please send me a man to fill those jeans."

Well, a short time later, the pastor of the church received a call from a very distraught mother. The woman told him about a weird thing her teenage son had started doing about a week earlier. She had gone into his room to tidy up and found a girl's bikini draped over one of his bedposts! The mom said she was very concerned.

It suddenly dawned on the pastor what was going on. The lady apparently had missed church the previous week; only her husband and son had attended. So, the pastor explained to the mom what her son was most likely doing.

There's a sense of truth in this humorous story. If we have a need for a Christian mate, and if we start praying over it consistently and fervently, God will meet that need in due time.

A word of caution: wait on God and don't get ahead of Him. If you're not careful, you will make a terrible mistake by giving into a spirit of desperation and not waiting patiently on God to answer your need. God will either answer on His timetable, or He will reveal why He isn't going to answer your request for a mate.

START ASKING

The third assignment I mentioned at the beginning of this chapter is asking God for daily strength. When you do, He will answer.

- You can ask Him to help you find a good Bible-teaching church, and He most assuredly will.
- You can ask Him to help you understand the Word of God or to help you choose a good Christian book that will provide you with godly counsel and feed your spirit.
- You can ask God to speak to you in the worship service and during the sermon at church, and He will.

Remember, you have not because you ask not.

The final divine assignment I mentioned earlier was to provide a living for your family. If you need a job, pray it into being. If you need a monetary raise, pray it into reality. If you are drowning in financial debt, ask God to show you the way out. Whatever you need relative to this task, you need to obtain through prayer.

There are many more divine assignments for you to discover and I pray this will stimulate your thinking process.

HOW GOD INTERVENES

If there's any one thing you must understand when you pray, it's that God resides in the spirit realm, and most everything He does is in that domain. According to John 4:24, "God is spirit, and those who worship Him must worship in spirit and truth."

God doesn't come out of the spirit realm into the physical very often, but when He does, we call it a miracle. It doesn't hurt to pray for miracles, but they aren't guaranteed. Let's look at how He works.

Say we start praying to God for a financial raise on the job. One way the Lord can intervene is that He can begin to move upon the spirit of our employer and start making him rethink what he's paying us. And the more we pray, the more he may feel guilty about our low wage and increase our pay. This is just one example of how God can move in our favor.

Another way He can operate is by putting a desire in the heart of the employers to sell the company to a larger firm that pays better wages—and He might do that just for you. Or He may place a desire in your heart to apply for a position in another company or firm—and in the process of changing jobs, you get a financial raise. Perhaps He might start showing you how you can cut corners and save money, which would accomplish the same objective.

Any way you look at it, when you begin praying, God starts moving in the spiritual realm. Also realize that sometimes it takes awhile for our prayers to be answered. People's minds and opinions are not changed overnight. God's Spirit has to have time to operate and work on the hearts of individuals. Every day you pray, He moves. And the days you don't, He might not. It's much like the parable where Jesus told a person to keep on knocking until he got what he wanted. Likewise, we must be persistent. Jesus explains this idea in two different passages.

First, look at Luke 11:5-9:

> Then He said to them, "Suppose one of you has a friend, and goes to him at midnight, and says to him, 'Friend, lend me three loaves; for a friend of mine has come to me from a journey, and I have nothing to set before him'; and from inside he answers and says, 'Do not bother me; the door has already been shut and my children and I are in bed; I cannot get up and give you anything.' I tell you, even though he will not get up and give him anything because he is his friend, yet because of his persistence he will get up and give him as much as he needs. So I say to you, ask and it will be given to you; seek, and you will find; knock, and it will be opened to you."

As I mentioned previously in this chapter, the word *ask* here in the Greek is in the present imperative tense, and it means to ask and keep on asking and don't stop until a manifestation of the answer appears.

Next read Luke 18:1-8:

> Now He was telling them a parable to show that at all times they ought to pray and not to lose heart, saying, "In a certain city there was a judge who did not fear God, and did not respect man. There was a widow in that city, and she kept coming to him, saying, 'Give me legal protection from my opponent.'
> "For a while he was unwilling, but afterward he said to himself, 'Even though I do not fear God nor respect man,

yet because this widow bothers me, I will give her legal protection, otherwise by continually coming she will wear me out.'"

And the Lord said, "Hear what the unrighteous judge said; now will not God bring about justice for His elect who cry to Him day and night, and will He delay long over them? I tell you that He will bring about justice for them quickly. However, when the Son of Man comes, will He find faith on earth?"

Notice that the evil judge soon comes to the conclusion that it's much easier to give the widow what she wants than to fight the unrest she is causing him. The discomfort of the people we are praying for will result from an invisible entity working from within, which is the Holy Spirit leaning hard upon their spirits. They won't even know why they are feeling this way.

GOD-SENT ANGELS

Many times each week I pray for individuals who are about to undergo some type of medical surgery. I pray that God will send an angel into the operating room with them and put thoughts and ideas into the hearts of the doctors and nurses as they perform the surgery. I ask that the Spirit of God will guide them, even supernaturally. Now obviously the physicians and the attending staff have skills and abilities and will think they came up with these possible lifesaving techniques, but in reality perhaps they would have never even thought of them if it hadn't been for our prayers and intercession. The Spirit of God is very powerful.

Angels can also be used by God to influence people. Satan is a fallen angel, so even he can affect the hearts of men and women. Take, for example, Acts 5:3, concerning Ananias and Sapphira. It tells us "But Peter said, 'Ananias, why has Satan filled your heart to lie to the Holy Spirit and to keep back some of the price of the land?'"

And also in Luke 22:3 we read, "And Satan entered into Judas who was called Iscariot..." The next thing you know, Judas is talking to the chief priests and officers as to how he could betray Jesus.

Thankfully, good angels also communicate with people. In Genesis 16:9-10, we read about Hagar, whom Sarai had treated harshly, causing Hagar to run away. The scripture records, "Then the angel of the Lord said to her, 'Return to your mistress, and submit yourself to her authority.' Moreover, the angel of the Lord said to her, 'I will greatly multiply your descendants so that they will be too many to count.'"

HELP FROM ABOVE

I love the story in Genesis 24 where Abraham tells his oldest servant to go to the land of his own country and find a wife for his son Isaac from his relatives. But the servant had some reservations regarding how to pull this off. "But what if she won't come back with me?" he asked. And here is Abraham's reply in verse 7: "The Lord, the God of heaven, who took me from my father's house and from the land of my birth, and who spoke to me and who swore to me saying, 'To your descendants I will give this land,' *He will send His angel* before you, and you will take a wife for my son from there."

Notice two aspects of this story. First, if you read on in this account, many things had to happen for this servant to be successful in the assignment Abraham gave him. But the mission was successful. Everything was made to order. Why? Because an angel from the Lord was working right alongside the servant, putting desires into the heart of Rebekah, as well as her parents. Without the angel's presence and his workings, this mission would not have been completed.

99

It's imperative for you to note that at no time did the servant visibly see the angel or have any clue as to his presence. Nevertheless, the angel was there.

The second thing I want you to see is Abraham's confidence. This guy really believed that the Lord would make this happen for him. Why? Because it was God's assignment that he raise a godly family, therefore, Abraham could move and pray with assurance.

God is always faithful to accomplish His will in our lives.

Angels can also speak to people in their dreams. In Genesis 31:11, it states, "Then the angel of God said to me in the dream, 'Jacob,' and I said, 'Here I am.'"

Psalm 34:7 is one of my favorite verses. It says the angel of the Lord encamps around those who fear Him and rescues them. *Encamp,* in the Hebrew, means "to settle down and set up camp."

The Bible also teaches that we all have guardian angels.

A Riverside Visitation

Something happened to me about fifteen years ago that I will never forget. I took a group of twenty college kids from our congregation to Oregon to visit another church. It took us about two days and two nights to get there. We traveled by vans in the daytime, and at night we stayed at a motel. Each evening, we would try to find a park or somewhere nearby where we could get alone and worship the Lord and have a Bible study.

On the second night, we arrived at the motel rather late, so we decided to send someone out for food while we started the worship and study time. We found a park setting and sent two of our chaperones (Chuck and Tonja) along with Josh, my son, to buy some burgers while we began our ministry session. After Chuck, Tonja, and Josh left, we discovered that there were too many people in the park setting we had chosen, so we decided to move down by the river a little farther from where we were staying. We ended up a pretty good distance away, on the opposite side of the motel.

Then, as Steve Tedder, who became our children's education pastor, began to lead us in worship music, the Holy Spirit touched me, and I fell into a kind of trance—a vision-like state of mind. I had never experienced this before nor have I since. It lasted for two to three minutes, and as the kids sang, I saw so clearly in my mind's eye probably twenty angels coming from all directions toward us. They approached mostly in twos and threes. Some came from the direction of the neighboring houses on the east side of the little park setting, others came up from the river, and some from behind me. They looked just like normal, young men clothed very generically.

Now, if it hadn't been for what occurred next, I would have probably thought my imagination was running wild, and I might not have known that these were angels. But as I slowly came out of this dream-like state, the first thing I consciously remembered were the words coming out of the mouths of our group, as they were singing. I especially remember Steve Tedder's voice as he sang, "He will give His angels charge over me. Jehovah Jireh cares for me, for me, for me. Jehovah Jireh cares for me!"

I immediately knew who those people were that I was seeing. They were God's angels. I stayed in a state of awe and reverence for the next couple of minutes and then lost sight of the angelic beings. I knew they were still all around us, but I was unable to see them anymore.

MINISTERING SPIRITS

I couldn't wait for there to be a break in the singing, so I could share with everyone what I'd seen. I wanted them all to hear this phenomenal story, but it dawned on me that Chuck, Tonja, and Josh weren't back yet. I also realized there was no way they were going to find us because they still thought we were at the park on the other side of the motel. So I prayed, "Oh, God, please get Josh, Tonja, and Chuck back here. In Jesus' name, Amen."

All of a sudden, I saw the angels again. They were standing around us as we sang. I saw one walk over to two other angels and tap them on the shoulder. He said something, and afterwards, they immediately left the group and headed into the street. I knew that they were going to get Josh, Tonja, and Chuck because of what I prayed.

It wasn't but ten minutes until the three headed toward us with our burgers and a story. Before I could utter a word after the singing was finished, Josh and Chuck exclaimed, "You won't believe how we found you guys. We prayed, and God supernaturally told us where you were."

It was amazing. I could hardly believe it. I was just given a glimpse of angels in action! Yes, they are real and do interact with us for our benefit. Hebrews 1:14 says of angels: "Are they not all ministering spirits, sent out to render service for the sake of those who will inherit salvation?"

So we have both the Holy Spirit, who is our helper, not the doer, working on our behalf when we pray, and we also have the angels of God.

PRAYING IN DIFFICULT CIRCUMSTANCES

When people come to me and ask me to pray over upcoming legal court dates, I usually pray, "God, please send an angel with them when they go to court, and cause the angel to speak into the heart of the judge, so he will hear and feel what You want him to know. Things he would be unaware of if we hadn't prayed this prayer. God, right now we believe that You've heard our cry, and whatever comes out of this judge's mouth tomorrow, we will accept with a spirit of joy and peace because Your will has been done. Amen."

Regarding our personal relationships, I also believe that God can put a desire of love back into our mate's heart for us, if we pray and continue to pray. His Spirit of love and forgiveness can override their seeds of hatred, unforgiveness, and bitterness. Now again, it's important for you to see that if, over the course of praying for love to be restored to the heart of an embittered mate, we start struggling with the request, then maybe God's trying to show us a different direction. But if the desire stays strong, and you feel an anointing when you pray for this, then don't stop until you see a manifestation of the request.

So ask the Lord to move in the spirit realm and do what He does best. He will place conviction into our unsaved loved ones' hearts to come to God. The more we pray, the more He'll activate His Spirit in their lives.

Pray that our children will be guided by the Spirit daily, to make wise decisions—choices that will keep them safe and secure. Continually ask the Lord that our sons and daughters will have a desire for God in their hearts on that particular day.

Ask the Holy Spirt to alert us to any potential danger that might threaten our families' well being, so we can pray it away. When we are seeking a physical healing, we should ask that God's Spirit will guide us to the right doctors and steer us away from anyone who might give us the wrong advice.

OBEY GOD'S PLAN

God divinely led me to reject my chemotherapy and to forego a bone marrow transplant, regarding my cancer. Now, keep in mind that there was a point in time when my doctors recommended both of these treatments, but God, through the promptings of the Holy Spirit, severely warned me to not take them. He told me that if I did, I would die. Now, in hindsight, I know I would have. Some others who were ill with leukemia at the same time as I was didn't know God or how to hear His voice, and they unfortunately died of their disease.

Please understand, I don't condemn anyone else who uses such treatments, because it's quite possible that God could choose to heal them through chemotherapy. God has a different plan for each person. I know people who testify to the fact that God used chemotherapy and bone marrow transplants to save their lives.

It's just that God knew my body—He made it, and He's intimately acquainted with every nerve, bone, and cell. He even knows the number of hairs on my head, and in His infinite wisdom, He knew these treatments would be toxic for my body, which brings me to my next point concerning prayer.

When we pray, we should always do so in the Spirit or as the Spirit guides us regarding what to say. I'm not against prayer lists, but subject your list to God daily, and let Him change it if He so desires.

START THINKING IN ADVANCE

Let me share an illustration of how I might pray in the Spirit for someone—say, a man I know—to come to Christ. On the first day I might ask God to start convicting him of his sin, and then thank the Lord for not only hearing this prayer but also for the action of conviction that begins as I speak.

The Apostle Paul taught us to always pray with a spirit of thanksgiving. After each time I approach God to do something, I immediately thank Him for already putting things into motion.

Then, on the second day, I might be led to continue with that same prayer, or I might not. Sometimes I feel the Holy Spirit convicting me to stick with one request for five or six days in a row. At some point, I might be led to start praying that God will inspire some influential Christian coworkers to start sharing Christ with him. And I could possibly pray that way for a day or maybe ten days.

Next, I might be led to pray for him to have a strong desire to go to church or to start being curious about the CDs I've given him or the Bible I sent to him. And one day, I may be led to take authority over the evil spirits that have blinded his mind. Whatever the Spirit leads me to pray, that's what I do.

ARE YOU LISTENING?

Prayer is a two-way communication hookup with God. We speak and let Him speak back to our hearts. It's similar to a telephone conversation between two close friends. We shouldn't do all the talking. Instead, we should allow Him to touch our innermost being as we converse.

Prayer is the avenue through which we get to know God's will. It is the way we get things done and draw closer to the Lord.

- Without prayer, we won't get much accomplished in life.
- Without prayer, our kids probably won't serve the Lord.
- Without prayer, we probably won't have a strong marriage.
- Without prayer, we can't be assured that God is watching out for our families.

Every morning and night, without exception, I pray over all of our kids, Debbie, and grandchildren—and I ask God to send His angels to be with them wherever they are, to guard them in all their ways. And should they find themselves in dangerous situations, I pray that God will manifest His angels and protect them. (Joshua had an angel manifest himself on a recent ski trip. I talk about it in *Conspiracy of Silence.*)

When any of our kids leave our mountain house, I ask God to send angels down to the freeway on-ramp and clear traffic for them. I then take authority over every demon and any plan they would have to inflict harm on my family, and I use my spiritual authority to command any of their schemes they may have concocted against my family to fail. I do all of this twice a day, and this keeps me from worrying.

BEAT THE DEVIL AT HIS GAME

Let me end this chapter by telling you that if prayer is as important as I've made it out to be, and I really think that it is, then be sure of this: Our spiritual enemy will do anything and everything he can to keep us from having the time or the desire to pray. He doesn't really care what it is that keeps us from calling on the Lord, just as long as it serves his purpose. He might try to make us feel unworthy to approach heaven. It's one of his favorite tricks to tell us that God won't hear our prayers or accept our praise because we are not worthy—we have too much sin in our lives.

Do you want to beat the devil at his game? Then the next time he whispers in your ear that you're unworthy, double your prayer time. I tell people that when you go to church you may hear that little voice in your inner being saying, "You can't worship God; you're too unclean. You are not worthy to raise your hands and praise Him, you hypocrite."

When this happens, we need to realize that we are all imperfect people, and even if there is sin in our life, we can still praise God. We should just lift up our dirty hands anyway and worship the Lord, because it's not about you and it's not about me. Worship is all about Him. He's worthy of our praise regardless of how we feel about ourselves. Sometimes we need to lift up our unclean hands and worship God in spite of ourselves.

Of course, if we're saved and have confessed our sins, we are clean before Him. It's a good idea to keep this in mind when we get into a feelings-oriented mood. Both the enemy and our flesh can use unworthiness as a tool to prevent us from praying.

ENDURANCE FOR THE RACE

Satan's demons will also try to keep you too busy to spend time with God. Ah ha! Some of you have no idea how the enemy operates. I dare you to go to God and lay all your commitments on the altar and ask Him to show you which ones are from Him and which are just things you've conjured up on your own. The enemy will use sinful addictions or just plain old habits that aren't beneficial, like watching some shows on TV for three hours a day, gabbing on the telephone every waking hour, or even spending extra time at your job. He doesn't care what it is, just as long as it accomplishes his objective to keep you from praying.

Hebrews 12:1 says, "Therefore, since we have so great a cloud of witnesses surrounding us, let us also lay aside every encumbrance and the sin which so easily entangles us, and let us run with endurance the race that is set before us."

Wherever we see a *therefore* in scripture, we need to ask ourselves what it's there for. It usually points to something in the previous chapter and connects it with the one that follows.

For example, Hebrews 12:1 refers us back to all the great men and women of faith mentioned in chapter eleven. Men and women such as Noah, Abraham, Sarah, Joseph, Moses, Rahab, Gideon, David, and Samuel. All these individuals were people of prayer and faith. They are the cloud of witnesses the writer of Hebrews refers to. They are our role models.

Abraham must have let his servants do a lot of the farming, so he could have time for God. Perhaps Noah took an early retirement from his profession, so he could make the will of God his number one priority and build the ark. Joseph didn't let the kingdom issues of Egypt take up all of his time. He had right priorities, and that's why it's said of him that he had a spirit of the divine God in him.

Hebrews 12:1 says we are to do what the cloud of witnesses already did—lay aside every encumbrance. An encumbrance isn't necessarily evil; it's just something that takes up and exhausts our time and energy.

And then we are told to lay aside the sin, which so easily entangles us. We all have one, don't we? This sin will keep us feeling too unclean to pray. It's a weight of guilt around our feet. And God wouldn't tell us to discard it if it was beyond our ability to do so.

Has the devil tricked you into not praying and spending time with God? Is Satan successful in your life?

KEEP ON ASKING AND BELIEVING

There are certain verses in the Bible that we should not ignore. James 4:2 says, "You lust and do not have; so you commit murder. You are envious and cannot obtain; so you fight and quarrel. You do not have because you do not ask."

Add to this what Jesus declared in Matthew 7:7-8: *"Ask,* and it will be given to you; seek, and you will find; knock, and it will be opened to you. For everyone who *asks* receives, and he who seeks finds, and to him who knocks it will be opened." And remember what He said in Matthew 21:22: "And all things you *ask* in prayer, believing, you will receive."

- Are you daily asking for divine help to live a life pleasing to God?
- Are you asking for spiritual strength for your kids?
- Are you petitioning God to watch over your family daily to protect them from all physical harm?
- Are you asking God to open doors, so you can share your faith?
- Are you asking for wisdom, so you can make right decisions?
- Are you asking for the ability to know when Satan is messing with your life?
- Are you asking for wisdom to understand the Word of God as you read it?

- Are you asking for divine help in controlling your thought life?
- Are you asking for help with your tongue?
- Are you asking for sensitivity regarding the needs of your family?
- Are you asking for divine strength to be a good employee?
- Are you asking for God's help in knowing what to eat and how to keep your body healthy?

What I want you to see is that American Christianity isn't taking the Word seriously. We need to wake up! If we don't ask, we're not going to have God's resources in our lives. The Lord has made asking a prerequisite to receiving. We need to repent of the sin of not praying and turn things around in our lives.

Tomorrow, set your alarm thirty minutes earlier than usual and begin reading the Word and start praying! You will be shocked at the difference it will make in your life.

James 4:8 says, "Draw near to God and He will draw near to you."

Six

A LEAP OF FAITH

Faith is like a muscle which grows stronger with use,
rather than rubber, which weakens when it is stretched.

— J. O. FRASER, MISSIONARY TO CHINA

Living by faith doesn't come naturally, and it isn't something we can pull off without remaining filled with the Holy Spirit. Philippians 4:13 tells us, "I can do all things through Him who strengthens me." This is where so many in American Christianity miss the message. It doesn't say, "I can do all things because I am a Christian."

Jesus expresses it even better in John 15:4-5: "Abide in Me, and I in you. As the branch cannot bear fruit of itself unless it abides in the vine, so neither can you unless you abide in Me. I am the vine, you are the branches; he who abides in Me and I in him, he bears much fruit, for apart from Me you can do *nothing.*"

I truly believe that living the life of faith is not possible without a deep commitment to remaining filled and drunk with the Holy Spirit. "And do not get drunk with wine, for that is dissipation, but be filled with the Spirit" (Ephesians 5:18).

Every morning when we get up, we make a choice concerning how close to God we want to live. If we choose to be really near to Him, then we must become filled with His Spirit at the start and remain that way the rest of the day. The Bible insinuates that we should become so filled that we are intoxicated with the Spirit. When someone is drunk, it is usually obvious because the liquor drives people to do, act, and say things they wouldn't normally do.

Have you ever driven down skid row and seen men standing on the corner acting kind of weird? If you stop and try to talk with them, you will immediately know that they are not quite right, something is obviously different about them. They're not acting normal. Why? They are intoxicated with wine. Their system is full of booze, and they can't help their behavior.

A BOLD STEP

The Bible teaches us that a common trait of being filled with the Holy Spirit is boldness. "But you will receive power when the Holy Spirit has come upon you; and you will be My witnesses both in Jerusalem, and in all Judea and Samaria, and even to the remotest part of the earth" (Acts 1:8). In other words, we will automatically find ourselves talking to people about the Lord and sharing our faith. We will not need to take five courses in Evangelism Explosion in order to know how to be a witness for God.

Ephesians 5:18 encourages us to become filled with God's Spirit. What follows in verses 19-21 is very important. It tells us to speak *"to one another* in psalms and hymns and spiritual songs, *singing and making melody with your heart to the Lord; always giving thanks for all things* in the name of our Lord Jesus Christ to God, even the Father; *and be subject to one another,* in the fear of Christ."

According to this passage, another trait of being filled with the Holy Spirit is wanting to minister to other Christians. We will have a desire to pick them up when they are down. We'll have no trouble at all praying with someone in the supermarket because we will be so concerned about them that the risk of being embarrassed won't even matter.

FULL AND RUNNING OVER

Have you ever had another Christian on your mind and then

111

later heard that something bad had happened to them, or find out that they had been going through a trial? Well, your burden for them was from God. He was trying to place the person on your heart, so you would pray for them.

So often we are called to be the answer to other people's prayers. I don't know about you, but more than once I have prayed, "Oh, God, I could really use some encouragement today." Now if any Christian is near me when I am expressing this, and they are filled with the Holy Spirit, then quite possibly they will hear God speaking to them to do or say something to encourage me. This is the way that God so often moves. To be filled with the Holy Spirit is to have the mind of Christ and the power of God's Spirit.

As a result of being filled with the Spirit, we'll be singing and making melody with our heart to the Lord. We can't be grouchy and complaining and also filled with the Holy Spirit at the same time. The two just aren't compatible.

So, the next time you encounter a grumpy Christian, just tell them that they need to be filled with the Holy Spirit. Let me illustrate my point this way. When a person bumps into someone else who is carrying a glass full of milk, most likely the milk will spill out of the glass. If the glass contains orange juice, then orange juice will spill out of the glass. If it's filled with Pepsi, then Pepsi will spill out of the glass. In the same way, if you are full of the Holy Spirit and someone bumps into you, joy, kindness, and grace should spill out of you.

Let me ask you a question: What has been spilling out of you the most this week?

Ephesians 5:19-21 also tells us that we will have a tendency to be thankful when we are filled with the Holy Spirit. Situations won't get us down like they do when we're not filled with His Spirit.

"IT'S NOT ME!"

For the two years my leukemia was most active, I found myself being the most happy and joyous that I had ever been. Looking back, it is no mystery to me as to why this was the case. Because of the threat of death and the need for divine intervention, I was staying really close to the Lord. I was constantly in the Word, and always praying and listening to praise music. I was keeping all sin and compromise out of my life. As a result, I was bubbling over with happiness and joy, and there were some who just couldn't understand why.

Often, people would come and tell me how much they admired me for my spirit of optimism and bravery. I would respond, "It's not me, it is the power of the Holy Spirit within me." In fact, I'd share with them that I had come to the conclusion that if we all lived as close to God as King David did when he was out in the field shepherding his father's sheep, then all of us would have had no problem taking on Goliath. The boldness to face the enemy would have automatically been there as a direct result of being filled with the Holy Spirit. In fact, I've told people many times that, regardless of the outcome of my battle with leukemia, I was thankful that God allowed it to come into my life because of how it motivated me to change spiritually.

A HEAVENLY PRESCRIPTION

Finally, in these verses we learn that a natural byproduct of being filled with the Holy Spirit is having a spirit of submission toward one another. We will have no problem recognizing God's voice and direction when it comes through other people. We will be totally at peace with our fellow believers and the role they play in our lives.

These three traits of being filled with the Holy Spirit—boldness, thankfulness, and submission to one another—are the same three characteristics depicted in the first three fruits of the Spirit in Galatians 5:22: love, joy, and peace. We love the brethren and minister to them out of love. We have joy in our hearts that manifests itself in singing and giving thanks. We have peace that comes from recognizing other giftings of the Holy Spirit in the body of Christ, and God's direction in our lives through them.

The other six traits of being filled with the Holy Spirit, according to Galatians 5:22-23 are patience, kindness, goodness, faithfulness, gentleness, and self-control. If we are lacking in these areas, it's a sure sign we're not filled with the Holy Spirit—and, as a result, we can't walk in faith.

By now, you should know if you're filled with God's Spirit or not. So often, we become filled with our own emotions and desires. If I go day after day without being filled with the Holy Spirit, I will quickly revert back to my pre-salvation character. It's not enough to have the Holy Spirit indwelling us; we must also strive daily to *be filled* with the Spirit.

We are all plagued with a disease called sin. The medicine that lets us live asymptomatically of sin's effects (producing or showing no symptoms) is the infilling of the Holy Spirit, reading the Word, and engaging in prayer. These are Dr. God's prescription for a healthy spirit and soul. If we obey Dr. God, we will be in good spiritual health, but if we fail to take our medicine, we will succumb to the symptoms of the disease of sin. Jesus hit the nail on the head when He declared, "We must abide in Him, or we can do nothing." I constantly encounter pessimistic Christians who have gone off of their medication!

FIVE STEPS TO THE SPIRIT

Allow me to tell you how to be filled with the Holy Spirit. This is a method I've used, and it is quite simple. You'll need a Bible, pen and paper, a CD player and headphones, plus a place where you can be alone with God for thirty or forty-five minutes.

First, pray and ask God to show you any active sin in your life. If He does, then confess it or agree with Him that it needs to go, and ask Him to fill you with the Holy Spirit.

Second, ask Him to show you what part of the Bible to read. Maybe you already have a chapter in mind. Begin to read with pen in hand, and when God speaks to you, either journal it or write out a note in your Bible.

Third, pray about everything God has placed upon your heart. This may include strength for yourself, for your family, for friends, and for divine protection. Thank Him for not only hearing your prayer but for what He is going to do as a result.

Fourth, ask Him to put people on your mind and heart. When He does, write their names in your notebook, so you won't forget. Then pray for them however the Lord directs. Write out what you prayed.

Fifth and last, end your alone time with God by listening to praise music for a few minutes. Before you leave, turn all your cares and worries over to Him. You can do this anytime during your prayer session. Believe that He will take your cares upon Himself. In 1 Peter 5:6-7 it tells us, "Therefore humble yourselves under the mighty hand of God, that He may exalt you at the proper time, casting all your anxiety on Him, because He cares for you."

THE GREAT TRANSFORMATION

As you leave your place of prayer, believe that you are filled with the Holy Spirit. After all, you have asked God in faith to fill you, and you have put action behind your prayers. So now most of your thoughts are going to come from the Holy Spirit. Why? Because you are filled with Him. It can be no other way.

Many think it's difficult to change how they are, but it's really not so hard at all. The devil wants us to believe this lie, so we won't even try. However, the way we change who we are is by changing what we think about.

If you are an angry person, it's because you are harboring angry thoughts. If you're suspicious or jealous, it's because you are allowing your mind to dwell on suspicious and jealous thoughts. The same is true with lustful thinking. If you watch lustful movies on television every night and go to bed thinking about immoral sex, then rest assured you will become more tempted as the days go by.

If you want to change the way you are, make a personal decision to start filling your mind with good, wholesome, biblically challenging thoughts. Read what Paul wrote in Philippians 4:8: "Finally, brethren, whatever is true, whatever is honorable, whatever is right, whatever is pure, whatever is lovely, whatever is of good repute (good report), if there is any excellence and if anything worthy of praise, dwell on and think about these things."

Obviously we have more control over our minds than we realize. Paul tells us in 2 Corinthians 10:5, "We are destroying speculations and every lofty thing raised up against the knowledge of God, and we are *taking every thought captive* to the obedience of Christ."

It's a truism that if you don't believe you can do something, then you won't even try. Succeeding may take some effort on your part, but we can't be afraid of work. A changed character will be well worth any sacrifice.

Just to prove that you can retrain your mind, let's conduct an experiment. Think for a minute or two about something negative someone has said about you in the past few years. Having done that, make a decision to think about a black and white horse skating on roller-skates down the street you live on. Think about that for thirty seconds. Now tell me what happened to the negative, possibly angry thoughts you had about the person who spoke ill of you? They disappeared, right? This is part of the process of renewing your mind—choosing good thoughts over bad.

GETTING STARTED

Focusing on what is right won't be difficult if you start rising every morning and filling your mind with the Holy Spirit. After you leave your quiet place with God, you'll be thinking about the people God has placed on your heart in prayer and how you can reach out to them. You will be remembering the verses you read and what they mean to your life. You'll be consumed with spiritual thoughts which will leave absolutely no room for negative concepts or ideas.

As your day continues during this mind-renewal process, be sure to safeguard against influences that can break the chain of spiritual thinking. Go through the CDs you have in your car and make sure they are edifying to your spirit. Now, I'm not suggesting they all have to be Christian praise music, but they shouldn't be lyrics that produce ugly, negative, lustful thoughts.

Throughout the day, plan for ways to reprogram your mind with wholesome thinking. Try carrying a good, thought-provoking Christian book with you so you can read it on your lunch and break time. Keep some uplifting sermon tapes or CDs (not sleepers) that you can play in the car as you drive. You might want to carry a prayer list with you, so when you have a spare moment, you can pray for individuals and cause kingdom work to be done as you travel about your day. You might have the phone numbers of some Christian friends programmed into your cell phone, so you can talk and receive the benefit of healthy fellowship as you drive around town.

These are suggestions to get you started. Before you go to bed at night, carefully choose the last things you'll be thinking about. Do all of this and you will be amazed at how fast your life will start changing. It all begins with being filled with the Holy Spirit.

AN INNER CONVICTION

Once you're filled with the Spirit, then we can talk about walking in faith. When Paul confronted a man named Elymas, who was trying to turn the proconsul away from the faith, Paul, who was "filled with the Holy Spirit, fixed his gaze on him and said, 'You who are full of all deceit and fraud, you son of the devil,

117

you enemy of all righteousness, will you not cease to make crooked the straight ways of the Lord? Now behold, the hand of the Lord is upon you, and you will be blind and not see the sun for a time.' And immediately a mist and a darkness fell upon him, and he went about seeking those who would lead him by the hand" (Acts 13:9-11).

Paul went out on a limb and did something that most rational thinking people would never dream of doing. He spoke out audibly what he thought the Holy Spirit would want him to say in this particular situation. He stepped out in faith and took a chance, and the results were astonishing. It was a spirit-of-awe thing!

Hebrews 10:38 says, "But My righteous shall live by faith; and if he shrinks back, My soul has no pleasure in him." And Hebrews 11:1 defines faith as "the assurance of things hoped for, the conviction of things not seen."

Faith is the inner conviction that you're going to receive something that, at the moment, doesn't seem possible. There is absolutely no evidence to lead you to believe that it will happen except for the strong feeling that is in your heart. Though it might look unattainable, deep inside you really know it will come about. Every time you pray, you believe strongly that it is going to happen.

This is called faith. It's the inner conviction that overrides the way circumstances look. Even though people tell you it won't materialize, your heart tells you differently.

CHECK YOUR MOTIVES

It's important to understand that what your heart is telling you should line up with scripture. It should be something you believe to be part of God's will for your life. You can't allow your inward feelings to mislead you. Again, if you are living right and in fellowship with God, if something in your heart is not of Him, it should dissipate over the course of a few days of praying.

James writes, "You ask and do not receive, because you ask with wrong motives, so that you may spend it on your pleasures (sensual delights)" (James 4:3).

Some people ask for the most ridiculous things. They pray for God to give them a very beautiful person as a mate, not concerned whether that individual is living a Christian life, assuming the outward beauty is a priority to God as much as it is to them, and the Lord says, "Oh, I don't think so."

While I believe we can ask God for anything, we need to qualify that it's part of His will. Boats, trains, and planes, as well as beautiful women and men, can be part of God's will, under the right circumstances.

One day as I prayed, God told me that He would give me anything I needed to accomplish His will in my life. If I needed a jet, He would provide it. If I needed homes in three countries, He would provide it. Whatever I needed to do His will, He would make a way for me to have it. But again, are these "things" in His will?

As we stay filled with the Holy Spirit, we will automatically become cognizant of certain needs and desires in life that coincide with God's plan. Once we become aware of these, we are to pray and ask the Lord to provide them for us. However, we shouldn't assume we'll get them just because we want them. God designed prayer as a way for us to reach out and set the process in motion. Once we pray for these heaven-approved desires and needs, we must then act as though we are going to receive them. This is the challenging part. When I had cancer, I had faith that God was going to keep me alive.

MORE THAN WISHFUL THINKING

What I'm going to share next is essential to understand in order to walk in faith as you are supposed to. You can't just conjure up faith. Some individuals have been taught to believe that a person can choose the things they want to believe God for, and that by choosing to believe in those things, they will come to pass. But no amount of believing will help you.

Someone might say, "I think I'll choose to believe that God will send a beautiful, sexy woman to become my wife. So starting today, I'm going to begin confessing, and acting as though Sally Jane will become my bride. After all, she's a Christian woman and she's my age, so I'm going to believe that it will become part of God's will for me."

This is what a well-meaning but misdirected Christian might believe, but it doesn't work that way. This is a biblically incorrect way of thinking and will not produce results. When you stop to think about it, this doesn't even make sense. Just because you desire this Christian woman doesn't necessarily mean that she wants you. What if she really goes out of her way to take care of herself, eat right, and exercise, but you are quite content with a little bit of a pudgy belly? You say, "What do looks have to do with anything?"

To her it may mean a lot, and she has the right to have a person in her life who has an equal desire to take care of his body as she does hers. God gave us the right to choose what we like and dislike. In addition, she might be praying for some other Christian man to become her husband with just as much faith as you are praying for her to become your wife. So before you go naming and claiming, make sure you have some inclination regarding God's will.

EXTRA BLESSINGS

How do we discover God's will? There are two ways. First, read His Word and search for what God's basic will is for your life. We know throughout the written Word of God that it's His plan for us to have our needs met. So we have to decide what a need is versus what is just a desire. There are a couple of scripture verses that tell us God will give us the longing of our heart, with some conditions.

Psalm 37:4 says to "delight yourself in the Lord; and He will give you the desires of your heart." The Hebrew for "delight" is *anog,* and it means to be soft, delicate, and dainty. So when people delight themselves in the Lord, they keep a soft, delicate heart toward Him. They are not stubborn, stiff-necked, or self-centered.

We would describe them as happy-go-lucky people. They love God so much that they only seek what He wants for their life. Their hearts are pliable and receptive, so when a desire presents itself, they immediately subject it to God. If He doesn't confirm in some way that this is from Him, they don't give it a second thought.

These individuals are so devoted to God that nothing they desire is so treasured that they can't live without it. But God loves to give favor to His obedient on-fire-for-God children with what I call "little extra blessings."

In this aspect, He is really no different than any other loving parent. He likes to bless obedient kids, and sometimes those blessings come through the desires of their heart. It's almost as if God looks down at us and says to Himself, "I am really pleased with that son or daughter's work. They are so passionate for Me. Let Me see if I can't give them some extra blessing today. What would really make them happy?"

So God inserts a desire into our heart—even though we may think it has originated with us.

Almost twenty-five years ago, Debbie and I started feeling the urge to become foster parents. So we began the process of getting licensed. After we were approved and were about to have an interview with our first two prospective foster kids, the thought hit me that I'd never asked God if we should do this. I just assumed that it would be His will.

So I immediately went to prayer, and in the course of my prayer time, I heard a little voice inside of me say, "Who do you think put the desire in your heart in the first place? I put it there. You didn't just conjure it up."

GET READY FOR AN ADVENTURE

The Holy Spirit guides us more often than we choose to believe. This is why it's so important for us to daily acknowledge all the things that happen in our lives and look for God in them. It's so exciting when we hand the controls of our life over to the Lord and watch Him move. Every day becomes an adventure.

One of my favorite scripture passages is Proverbs 3:5-6: "Trust in the Lord with *all* your heart, and *do not lean on your own understanding. In all your ways acknowledge Him,* and *He will* make your paths *straight"*.

I know far too many Christians who don't recognize God in all their ways, and they fail to pray about everything in their lives. First Peter 1:13 says, "Therefore, prepare your minds for action, keep sober in spirit..."

Remember, we are the only body God has on this earth, so when He wants something done, He will choose to do it through you and me. Every day God wants to accomplish things in our world. Through us He wants to speak, touch, help, encourage, warn, and save people—all with our help.

Spirit-filled and Spirit-led Christians have hopefully learned to sense God's touch and hear His voice in their inner spirits, but the rest of the world and immature Christians need to experience God through physical bodies. They don't have the capability of making contact with Him in the spirit realm, so when God wants to do a work in your neighborhood, guess who He wants to use to do it? Yep, you and me.

So many Christians are twiddling their thumbs with nothing to do. Obviously they don't get the idea of *servanthood Christianity*. They have totally missed the whole concept of kingdom living.

When God wants to do something on earth, He first puts the

desire in our hearts that coincides with His plan. When we consult God to determine if this desire is from Him or not, He will usually answer with a confirmation of some sort. That is, He will give us an outward or inward sign that this is His will for our life.

He might have your pastor speak on the topic that you're wrestling with, and this will serve as a sign. Or maybe He will have a friend call you with a verse that goes right along with that desire. He might even just start bugging you daily with a more than usual intensity concerning the issue at hand. Whatever way He uses to confirm this desire is from Him, it will become pretty obvious that this is more than an ordinary longing.

A NEW CHALLENGE

Several years ago, I started experiencing a feeling of unrest in my spirit. I didn't feel content to just stay at the church in Bakersfield and do the same-ol', same-ol' every week. I felt I could do so much more for the Lord than what I was doing. After all, we now had eleven full-time pastors on staff, not counting a lot of part-time help.

I began feeling that perhaps I should pastor people in another city, as well as Bakersfield. We were having such a great success in the Bakersfield church, seeing people's lives totally changed by the power of the Holy Spirit that I began wanting to share the same message with people in another city who possibly were not being fed spiritually.

This desire slowly began to intensify into a strong calling. So I prayed about it for months. One day, when Debbie and I were out on our daily walk, I came to the conclusion that this burden wasn't going to go away until I moved out on faith and did something about it.

Often people seek God too long over issues. They pray beyond a point that they should pray. I believe that prayer can become a sin when you begin to substitute it for action. There can come a time when God says, "I don't want you to pray about this anymore. I want you to act in accordance with your faith. Stop praying and start doing."

In Exodus 14, the children of Israel were coming out of Egypt, where they had been living in bondage and captivity for decades. God was in the process of supernaturally leading them out of Egypt with Moses as their leader. The Egyptian army was in hot pursuit. They had no intentions of letting the people of God go. As the Israelites ran from the Egyptian armies, they came to a dead end. With mountains on each side of them and the Red Sea in front of them, they were boxed in.

Moses began to pray to God while the armies drew closer and closer. Finally God said, "Why are you crying out to Me? Tell the sons of Israel to go forward" (v. 15). In other words, "Stop praying and start doing."

Is there something you have been praying about for a long, long time that you believe is God's will, but nothing has happened? Well, just maybe it's time to stop praying and turn to action.

WHY NOT BOISE?

This is where I was with my desire to plant another church. So when Debbie and I got back from our walk, I sat down in my big chair, pulled out a map, and started looking at cities. I prayed, "God, please lay a city on my heart." And when He didn't, I just chose one.

I yelled out to Debbie, "Pack your suitcase; we're going to Boise, Idaho."

"Why?" she asked.

"I'm not sure," I replied. "I just want to get out of town and start exploring areas where we can pioneer a church."

"Why Boise, Idaho?" she wanted to know.

All I could reply was "Why *not* Boise, Idaho? At least it's a place to start."

See, I've come to understand a principle over the years and that is sometimes God won't move until we do. Much of the time we think we are waiting on God, when in fact He is waiting on us. So we packed our bags and set out for Boise. We drove as far as Reno, Nevada, that night and checked into a hotel room. We resumed our journey the next day. As we drove into Boise, I immediately knew that this wasn't the place we were supposed to be, but we drove into the city anyway, grabbed a bite to eat, and headed out of town.

WAS IT RENO?

Well, we drove back into Reno that night, checked in at the same place we stayed before, and settled down for the evening. I still remember that as we sat in the hotel room and looked over the city lights, I prayed a very simple prayer: "God, I'm confused. Please show me where you want me to pioneer a church. I'm doing it for You and not for me."

All of a sudden a verse popped into my mind. I opened my Bible and read a passage that dealt with a very immoral city with sinful people. I thought it could refer to Reno, Nevada, and I began to get excited because I love mountain towns with big trees, streams, and lakes. I thought, "God, You're too good. I've always lived in a desert, agricultural town, and now my dream is going to come true."

I told Debbie that we needed to hurry and get to sleep, so we could wake up early the next day and start looking for buildings.

As you can see, I'm not one to let too much grass grow under my feet. I'm rather impulsive by nature. It's a wonder God can even use me. I have the bad habit of talking to God, and when He starts telling me something really exciting, I run off in the middle of the conversation and start acting upon the little that I heard. I very seldom let the Lord finish a conversation with me. It's like God says, "Ron, I have a great work for you to do."

I reply, "Yes, God, I'm all ears."

And when God continues with, "I want you to go to Reno, Nevada and..." I cut in with, "I hear you Lord. I'm out of here. I'll pioneer a church in Reno, Nevada. Yes, I will." And I take off and start making a fool of myself when all along God was going to say, "I want you to go to Reno, Nevada, get a room there and seek me. Then I will tell you where I want you to pioneer a church."

Poor God, He has to put up with the likes of you and me. And when we make a mess out of things, He has to spend time repairing the damage!

"THE HIDDEN PLACE"

Well, we drove all over Reno the next day looking for buildings. We went home with a few leads, but nothing too promising. On the way back, Debbie said something I didn't want to hear: "Ron, I know you're going to think I am crazy, but I don't think God's telling us to pioneer a church in Reno, but I do think He is telling us to go to Las Vegas, Nevada and start a ministry there."

I couldn't believe my ears because Debbie has always hated Las Vegas. I mean when we travel through there, she won't even let me stop and get gas. Was I really hearing this come from my wife? It wasn't agreeable with me. I wanted majestic mountains and streams and lakes. Vegas? No way. So we continued back to Bakersfield.

Debbie tried to convince me to just drive through Vegas, but I wouldn't have any of it. We headed straight home. But God started working on my heart and wouldn't let up.

"Vegas, Vegas, Vegas." It was on my mind constantly. I began to look up statistics about the city. I even learned some of the history behind it. I found out that in the early days, many bad guys would go there to hide out from the law and that one nickname for it was "the hidden place."

I wasn't quite ready to throw my hat over the fence, but God certainly had my attention. It all came together one night when I was called to the hospital to pray for a newly born baby who was not expected to live. As I sat in the waiting room with another couple from our church, the wife looked over at her husband and said, "Here's your chance to give Pastor Ron those verses you've wanted to share with him." And he handed me some passages that basically said God was calling me to a desert land—a dry place that was once hidden and that I would be successful there.

It blew me away. This described Las Vegas to a tee. God had gone out of His way to confirm His call for me to go to Vegas and start a church. This man had no idea how important these verses were to me.

I use this illustration to show you that confirmations don't have to be way out there or spectacular. Here's what I had: A strong desire in my wife's heart that wouldn't go away; a strong desire in *my* heart that wouldn't leave, which became stronger when I prayed; the verses God had given me in the hotel room in Reno; and the verses given to me in the hospital waiting room. This was enough for me to realize that God was calling me to Vegas.

THE RIGHT STEP

Following God's calling, we went to Las Vegas, found a building, and signed a $750,000 lease for five years. Then I got depressed!

I didn't know a single soul in that city. All I had to go on was what I believed to be a calling and promise from God. I was totally walking by faith. I felt it in my heart strongly but had no evidence whatsoever of anything that would support that feeling.

Thank God, the venture has been one hundred percent successful. We've never been unable to pay a bill, and the church is growing rapidly.

I have now turned the church over to my son-in-law, who was one of the main Lead Pastors on the California campus.

When will we learn that God is faithful? *When we step out in faith and do His will.* Most people don't have a testimony because they've never taken a risk, stepped out in faith, or have done something they felt God wanted them to do.

OUT ON A LIMB

Earlier I alluded to the fact that God gives us divine faith when He wants to accomplish His purpose in our lives. When God wants something done and He wants to do it through us, He does two things. First, He puts a desire into our hearts, and second, He gives us faith to believe that desire will come to fruition. As I said earlier, faith cannot be conjured up. It has to be placed into our hearts supernaturally by God.

Read what Romans 10:17 has to say on the subject: "Faith comes from hearing, and hearing by the word of Christ." Now the Greek word used here for 'word' is *rhema.* A rhema is a personal word that God speaks to you. It's like a promise with your name written on it. It's when He goes out of His way to communicate that He's speaking something special to us—and somehow in our hearts we know it. God can speak rhemas to you in many ways.

There are times you can hear rhemas in a sermon. Have you ever been to church and felt like the pastor was talking just to you, as if you were the only one in the building? This is God speaking a *rhema* to you. That sermon had your name written all over it.

Perhaps you read a verse in the Bible that you can't get out of your head? Like it jumped off the page and into your heart when you read it, and it won't go away. That's God speaking to you.

Or have you ever had two or three things happen that all seem to carry the same message with them? This is usually God also. So when the Lord births faith in your heart that is specific and it won't go away, this is when you have to take what I call the leap of faith. You have to go out on a limb and take action in accordance with that faith.

As James asks, "What use is it, my brethren, if someone says he has faith but he has no works? Can that faith save him? If a brother or sister is without clothing and in need of daily food, and one of you says to them, 'Go in peace, be warmed and be filled,' and yet you do not give them what is necessary for their body, what use is that? Even so faith, if it has no works, is dead, being by itself " (James 2:14-17).

DIVINE SEEDS

If you fail to act on your faith in a reasonable amount of time, it will die on you. It has a very short shelf life. In Matthew 13, we have the parable of the sower that contains a principle I believe relates to what James said. That is, God plants His seeds into the hearts of people. The Greek word for "seed" is *sperma*. It is where we get our English word for sperm. It's the substance that can impregnate a female.

When you hang around with God and become very intimate with Him, it would be natural for Him to plant His seeds into your heart, impregnating you with ideas, ministries, good works, and deeds.

If you are fertile, healthy soil, and you receive these seeds (sperma) as divinely given by God, and you pray over them and act upon them, at the proper time they will give life to others. But if you receive these seeds and keep them inside of you for a long period of time, and never give birth to anything in the kingdom realm, they will die and become petrified within you. Sooner or later the seed will be aborted.

I can't count how many Christians I have come across in my lifetime who have been called by God to do mighty works, but they have let all those great seeds die within them. They never acted upon the desires and faith that God placed in their heart and soul.

It has been said that some of the greatest untapped riches in the world lie in the cemetery. I believe that God has called many of you who are reading this book to do awesome things for Him and

His kingdom, but you've never acted on your faith. You have never thrown your hat over the fence. As a result, the calling, the faith, and the desire have withered and died. As Matthew said in the parable of the sower, the devil stole the seed. You let the shelf life of the vision expire.

I don't say this to discourage you, but to teach and motivate you to not be hesitant. I want to encourage you to step out in faith and do something when you have enough confirmations to know that a calling is from God.

Abraham didn't wait around a day or two when he was called to offer Isaac as a sacrifice. "Now it came about after these things, that God tested Abraham, and said to him, 'Abraham!' And he said, 'Here I am.' He said, 'Take now your son, your only son, whom you love, Isaac, and go to the land of Moriah; and offer him there as a burnt offering on one of the mountains of which I will tell you.' So Abraham rose early in the morning and saddled his donkey, and took two of his young men with him and Isaac his son; and he split wood for the burnt offering, and arose and went to the place of which God had told him" (Genesis 22:1-3).

Abraham was off and running the next morning. He didn't procrastinate. In the New Testament, we are told that Abraham is our example of faith: "The righteous man shall live by faith" (Galatians 3:11).

What a testimony it is to the world when we act upon our expectation and belief, and as a result, amazing things happen. We need to continually show those around us what takes place when a person puts their faith in God.

THE BIRTH OF FAITH

My cancer was a real eye-opener to many. When I stood on faith and assurance that God would be faithful to the words He had given me, the world around me watched and waited to see if God was real—to see if He would come through for me. When He did, many had to reevaluate their thoughts and opinions about the Lord. Living by faith requires some risk-taking. Once you find out that God won't let you down, it will change your life forever.

I preached at a pastor's camp years ago on the subject of faith. When I returned, a few years later, I was standing in the sanctuary during a time of worship and this guy across the way, who was holding a baby, kept smiling and nodding at me. I smiled and nodded back. After the service, he came up to me and said, "See this baby? You're the reason we have him."

He went on to explain that when he and his wife were at the camp years earlier, they had given up on having kids because they were told that it just couldn't happen to them. But when he heard my sermon, God birthed faith into their hearts, and they decided to take a stand and believe God for the impossible. Their beautiful little son was the result.

TOTAL FORGIVENESS

You can pray all you want, but there will come a time when you will have to put some feet on your prayers. Prayer was never meant to be an end itself. It's not a duty to perform so that we can receive brownie points in heaven. Rather, it is a way to see things accomplished.

I believe that weekly we ought to write on a notebook at least two or three things that God has placed upon our hearts while in our prayer closets. And then as the week progresses, we need to act upon them to some degree to see if they have been put there by God. The only way we are going to learn to walk in the Spirit is by experimenting. Christians should never have a problem with inactivity.

Try this. Go into your prayer closet tonight and confess every sin you can think of. Get right with God, and spend some time telling Him how sorry and repentant you are. After you confess, choose to believe that He's forgiven you, no matter what your conscience tells you.

Recently, I was in Las Vegas preaching when I saw someone who reminded me of my former self. I began to think about my past life prior to my salvation. I even began to recall some of the sinful things I did when I was in the early years of my ministry. And I really began to feel condemned and unworthy to be in the ministry. I began to pray, "God, You know I've never meant to hurt You or the cause of Christ. In fact, the sins that I feel so convicted about were committed in the line of duty. I didn't go out and look for sin, I just fell victim a few times to the ploys of the enemy, and I feel so sorry that I did. I pray today that You will look at all the good things I've done in my life and not remember my failures. I have given my time to the poor and the hurting, and I've tried to be loving and patient with all the people You have placed in my path. I have never been ashamed to do or say what You've wanted me to, no matter what the consequences. Oh, God, today I beg You to speak to me personally and tell me that You have truly forgiven me of all my sins and that You don't even remember them any more. This would mean so much to me..."

Before I could finish the prayer, Isaiah 43 flashed across my mind over and over again, to such a degree that I pulled off the freeway to read it. Now, after walking with God in a very intimate way for all these years, I really can sense when He wants to speak to me. Once I pulled off the freeway, I quickly turned to Isaiah 43 and kept saying to myself how awesome and miraculous it would be if there were something in this chapter about my sins that was just for me. I read with great anticipation and could hardly contain my excitement when I read Isaiah 43:25-26: "I, even I, am the one who wipes out your transgressions for My own sake; and I will not remember your sins. Put Me in remembrance, let us argue our case together; state your cause, that you may be proved right."

I was so thrilled. Not only had God heard my prayers and specifically answered them, but He also heard my explanation and my reasoning as to why I wanted Him to forgive me.

God really does hear the prayers of His children. He

encourages us to pour our hearts out and tell Him what we feel and why. God loves transparency.

WRITTEN ON YOUR HEART

Let's get back to our experiment. Confess your sins before God and plead your case before Him. Don't make excuses for your sins, because we have none. Just tell Him how you feel, and then let Him know that in spite of it all, you're really sorry for all your failings and agree with Him that they are a wrong approach to life. Then believe that He has heard your prayers and has forgiven you.

Next, ask Him to put a name or face of someone on your heart. When He does, write that person's name in your notebook. Then pray whatever God tells you concerning that person.

Pray for this individual every day, and then call and tell him or her what you prayed for. This will lead you right into ministry. You sure won't have to worry about being bored. God never runs out of people to pray for and minister to. Practice this starting today, and I promise you will be blown away when you see all the fruit that it can potentially produce.

We must learn to see the prayer of faith as a way for seeing kingdom business accomplished. It's not just some passive activity we do to tell God that we put in our time just like a good Christian should:

• Pray to get things done or don't pray at all.
• Pray to hook up with God or don't pray at all.
• Believe in what you pray or don't pray at all.

Every time you come out of your prayer closet, you should be convinced that you've taken care of God's business—that you have started some activity in the angelic realm.

Someone once told me that to make his prayer life more effective, he brought a chair into his prayer closet and visualized

God's presence seated before him. He said this motivated him to stay more focused.

If that sort of thing helps, then go for it! Just realize that God hears and is ready to answer your every prayer. And after you pray, you have to live as though God not only heard those prayers, but is going to answer them, when they are prayed according to His will.

WHAT DOES THE WORD SAY?

Let me remind you that it's not difficult to know if something is of God. There are two simple ways to find out. First, does it line up with God's Word? For example, when I pray for forgiveness of sins, I know it's His will for me to be forgiven, simply because it says so in 1 John 1:9 and in other places in scripture. So after I pray and ask for forgiveness, I need to act forgiven and quit walking around with my head down. Or, for instance, if I ask God for wisdom concerning a need I have in my life, then when I finish praying, I need to start living according to my heart because I received wisdom from God. It says in James 1:5, "But if any of you lacks wisdom, let him ask of God, who gives to all generously and without reproach, and it will be given to him."

Remember, when you become filled with the Holy Spirit, you should expect to receive power. And when you pray for the healing of others, you should expect them to get better because the Word of God tells you what His will is regarding this.

You need to study the Bible for yourself in order to find what the will of God is. When you tithe ten percent of your money to the church, you should expect all the blessings of Malachi 3:10. When you give up something in the physical realm in order to fulfill God's will, you should expect to be blessed for doing that because of what Jesus said in Mark 10:29-30: "Truly I say to you, there is no one who has left house or brothers or sisters or mother or father or children or farms, for My sake and for the gospel's sake, but that he will receive a hundred times as much now in the present age, houses and brothers and sisters and mothers and children and farms, along with persecutions; and in the age to come, eternal life."

One of our pastors was telling me a few months ago how someone had blessed him with a new bicycle, and as I was expressing my joy for him, it suddenly dawned on me that some months earlier he had given a bike away. When I brought this to his attention, we were both blown away. Now needless to say the law doesn't always work out exactly this way, but it can. I once gave a car to a person in need, and I believe as a direct result of that, I have a God-story behind almost every vehicle I've bought in the last twenty years. It is really quite amazing when you start analyzing how divine laws work.

Most Christians are overlooking many interesting principles and truths in God's Word—which cannot lie. Yes, you will discover His will by knowing His written Word, and once you receive it, live accordingly, then it will become reality. It's all so simple yet many in AC have missed it.

No More Confusion

Let me reiterate that the second way to know God's will is to take something before God in prayer and pray over it for ten to fifteen days. If it is of God, then your desire and passion for that area of life will grow and stay intensely heavy on your heart. On the other hand, if it is not God's will, your desire and passion will begin to dissipate.

Although I know that to some this method sounds a bit risky, I have found it to be tried and true in my life, but only if I have prayed hard over these issues for consecutive days.

In John 14:16-17, 20, Jesus says this about the Holy Spirit, "I will ask the Father, and He will give you another Helper, that He may be with you forever; that is the Spirit of truth, whom the world cannot receive, because it does not see Him or know Him, but you know Him because He abides with you and will be in you... In that day you will know that I am in My Father, and you in Me, and I in you."

Also in John 16:8, Jesus teaches concerning the Holy Spirit: "And He, when He comes, will convict the world concerning sin and righteousness and judgment."

In addition, Colossians 3:15 tells us, "Let the peace of Christ rule in your hearts, to which indeed you were called in one body; and be thankful."

By these verses, you can conclude that you are able to know God's will. He never leaves you in a state of confusion.

The Apostle Peter writes in 2 Peter 1:3 that God has granted us everything we need pertaining to life and godliness. So once you know God's will, you must line up your life with it. Act as if you believe that what God says will happen. Act upon your convictions, and as you do, you will begin to see the manifestations of those promises come true. It's nothing short of mindboggling. You will begin to develop a new appreciation for God's Word. God cannot and does not lie. Romans 1:17, says, "For in it the righteousness of God is revealed from faith to faith; as it is written, *'but the righteous* man *shall live by faith.'*"

And in Hebrews 11:6 we read, "And without faith it is impossible to please Him, for he who comes to God must believe that He is and that He is a rewarder of those who seek Him."

So put feet to your prayers and watch God move miraculously in your life. It's a very counter-cultural way to live, but it is the biblical way. What do you have to lose?

I believe this leap of faith will alter your future forever.

Seven

THE HEART
OF THE MATTER

*If we could read the secret history of our
enemies, we would find in each man's life sorrow and
suffering, enough to disarm all hostility.*

– HENRY WADSWORTH LONGFELLOW

WARNING: THIS CHAPTER MAY BE OFFENSIVE
TO SOME, SO PRAY BEFORE YOU READ IT.

Maybe you've heard the pop song from the sixties, "What the world needs now is love, sweet love." The lyrics go on to say, "It's the only thing that there's just too little of."

I agree. In today's church world, we have many activities going on but so little love. I was in a total state of disbelief a few years ago when one of the major denominations asked all of its members to boycott one of the major theme parks because they hire gay people. I thought that's really going to lead them to the Lord and show them the love of God, isn't it? I mean, why don't we just boycott every place that hires unbelievers. We could pass a kingdom law that says Christians can only patronize businesses that other Christians own. "Christians hang with Christians" could be one of our new bumper stickers. "God Hates Sinners" could be another—and don't forget to include in bold brazen letters, "Especially Gays."

No wonder people are not coming into our churches and being

saved or turning to us when they need help. Perhaps we should all go back to our Sunday School days and re-memorize John 3:16: "For God so loved the world (gays included), that He gave His only begotten Son, that whoever (gays and lesbians included) believes in Him shall not perish, but have eternal life."

Some believers need to be retrained, and some men of war who still exist in the church need to retire. In all of our campuses, you will find a few *traditional* people. I love these individuals, but some of them have been poisoned by the traditional church world and need to be retrained.

In the Vegas church, we used to have a soup kitchen downtown at the mission. Every Sunday, we would feed the homeless. One day, we brought an ex-stripper with us who had been saved a couple of weeks earlier. Admittedly, she wasn't dressed very appropriately according to "church standards," but I've seen worse. While I was in the back of the mission talking with a volunteer, one of our parishioners came in and said, "Pastor, some of our people are in the back room discussing who should approach the ex-stripper sister about her inappropriate dress. You might want to intervene."

So I took these concerned Christians aside and told them that we needed to give her some grace—after all she was trying to do something good with her life now. "Give her credit for at least being down here," I told them.

"But what about the men she is serving?" someone asked. "She could be a stumbling block."

I had to smile. "We are in Las Vegas," I told them. "Believe me, this lady isn't showing them anything they don't see a dozen times a day."

We so often strain out a gnat and swallow a camel. We are more worried about the way people are dressed than we are with their eternal salvation.

TATTOOS? IN CHURCH?

At Valley Bible Fellowship, we have a smorgasbord of people.

In fact, we attract a lot of individuals with tattoos. For some reason, tattooed people seem to like us. Recently I received a letter from a fellow pastor in our community who works with youth. In it, he admonished me for allowing young people, after getting saved, to keep their tattoos. He included the old favorite verse of all tattoo-haters found in Leviticus 19:28: "You shall not make any cuts in your body for the dead, nor make any tattoo marks on yourselves."

I hear this verse quoted quite a bit, but those who quote it fail to realize that these laws were written for the Jewish people in the Old Testament and really don't pertain to us today. Now, before you object too strongly, I encourage you to go back and read the book of Leviticus, and while you're reading it, pay attention to the verse that comes right before the tattoo verse—Leviticus 19:27. It reads: "You shall not round off the side growth of your heads nor harm the edges of your beard."

Maybe the tattoo-haters are hypocrites! After all, I've seen some of them, and they don't even have beards. Heaven forbid, they have harmed their whole face. And if you're baldheaded, you better check out all the Levitical rules about having a bald head. And if you're a fruit lover you need to check out Leviticus 19:23: "When you enter the land and plant all kinds of trees for food, then you shall count their fruit as forbidden. Three years it shall be forbidden to you; it shall not be eaten."

I wonder who's counting the years, and I wonder if we are obligated, when we go to the grocery store, to ask the produce clerk if he could find out the age of the tree from which we are buying fruit. I'm sure he would be impressed with our question!

I don't mean to be cantankerous, but I'll admit to being a little frustrated with people who miss the big picture. (And by the way, I don't have any tattoos.)

THE STONE THROWERS

We need to love the world. I don't think we should condone

139

their sin at all, but I believe we can love them without doing that. I haven't always felt this way; I guess time and grace has mellowed me. I find it difficult to throw stones at sinners—perhaps it's because I find myself being one more often than I'd like to admit.

I knew God was really doing a work in my life several years ago when two brothers in the Vegas church and I went street-witnessing. We came across a group of people on a side street who were gathering for the start of a parade. So we decided to go over and check it out. It ended up being the annual gay and lesbian parade. I suggested that we watch what was happening and see if any ministry opportunities presented themselves. I also wanted to educate myself with the Las Vegas culture. The parade was, needless to say, filled with blatant immorality and debauchery. But as I stood on the road and watched these people flaunt degradation and sin, I felt something well up in my soul I'd never experienced before—the love and compassion of Christ for these men and women.

Ten years earlier, I would have probably pulled my sanctimonious collar up and demanded that we leave this damned place of sexual indulgence and blasphemy. But not this time. Something was different. Tears began to form in my eyes, and I momentarily felt like running out into the street to tell these people how much God loved them and wanted to save them from their sins—how much He longed to give them a life of joy and peace. (Something they obviously weren't finding.)

I'm presently in a state of spiritual healing from my past life of traditional churchism, so I won't be too hard on everyone. I'm in the process of becoming free enough to walk up to the streetwalker on the sidewalk, smile, and start a conversation with her, if God so leads me—without worrying what the fellow Pharisees may think of me.

Who smiles at the streetwalker without wanting some sexual favor from her? How many Christians approach and start a conversation with a Hells' Angel if they come across one? How often do we hold a door for a bunch of punk rockers at the shopping mall, or do we automatically think in our subconscious minds that these kids aren't worth the effort? I wonder just how prejudiced and segregated we are in the recesses of our minds where no one sees.

GERALD AND JOHN

Once, while I was down at the Vegas city mission, two street people came up and were talking to one of the brothers of the church after the service. One guy was white, the other was black, and they were really, really dirty and unkempt in appearance. My heart immediately went out to these two men, and I began a conversation with them. Soon I felt the Holy Spirit begin to tug at the strings of my heart. I felt Him telling me to take these guys back to the California church and help them. So I blurted out, "I want to take you guys home with me to California."

Debbie, who was standing nearby, heard what I said. She tugged on my coat and whispered, "Ron, you're not seriously going to take these guys home with us are you?"

And I replied, "Yep."

She was a little more than uncomfortable with this situation, like most women would be. So, I ended up giving them some money and told them to catch a bus the next day. I said we would meet them at the bus depot in California.

Debbie told me she didn't think I would ever see them again, after giving them cash for their ticket. But I bet on them simply because not many people treated them as if they had value. Even though I had just met them, I trusted them. I chose to believe in them and guess what? They didn't let me down. They both showed up in California. We'll call them Gerald and John to protect their identity.

Gerald was an African-American, and John was a good ol' white boy from Oklahoma. They stayed with us for a few weeks, and then John went back to Oklahoma. Gerald went to Teen Challenge in Riverside. Although I didn't hear much more from John after he left, Gerald and I remained close for some time. He still thanks God every time I see him for helping him get off the streets and get his life right with God.

When these guys came into our lives, we didn't spend a lot of time trying to indoctrinate them. We just loved on them and helped them get jobs, a home, and a car. We figured that Christian values would automatically come as we spent more time with them, sharing the Word of God. The writer James tells us, "Pure and undefiled religion in the sight of our God and Father is this: to visit orphans and widows in their distress, and to keep oneself unstained by the world" (James 1:27).

More than likely you've heard the saying, "The world doesn't care how much we know, until they know how much we care." How true.

A McDonald's Prayer Line

One winter morning, on my way to the Children's Hospital in Fresno, California, I decided to pull off the freeway, in a little town along the way, to get a quick breakfast at a McDonald's.

There was a long line at the restaurant, and as I stood there, many people began to complain. But because I was filled with the Holy Spirit that morning, I just stood there and smiled. Soon, the lady behind me tapped me on the shoulder and asked, "How come you are so different than everyone else?"

Her question took me by complete surprise. Was I? "Well, it's probably because I'm in love with God, and I don't have a lot to complain about," I replied.

"I knew it," she said. "I just knew that you were a Christian." She asked me where I was going, and I told her I was a pastor and that a child from our church was sick in the hospital in Fresno.

Immediately, she asked if she could pray for me—right there in the McDonald's line. So we did. She prayed for me, and I for her, unashamedly, the way it should be. Needless to say, some in the line got a little upset because we held things up for a few seconds, but that's okay. It meant a lot for the lady to pray for me.

I felt in my heart that this was some sort of breakthrough for her. I paid for my food and sat down. She took her meal to a table about six spots away from mine. As usual, I prayed over my food, and as I did, God seemed to be speaking to my heart. "Go give that lady $80 bucks."

For a moment I hesitated, thinking, "Nah, this isn't God. This is just my imagination."

But the thought kept growing, and it got stronger and stronger. So finally I prayed, "God, if this is You, then cause her to still be there when I get through with my breakfast."

I think I ate slower than usual that morning. When I finally was finished, she was still there, of course. I went over and said, "Excuse me, but I really feel like God wants me to give you this forty dollars." Keep in mind that God said eighty, but I was being a cheapskate.

She began to weep, and confided, "You know, I've been out all morning delivering newspapers. I took this extra job because neither one of my kids have coats to wear to school, and just today I asked God to help me. Thank you soooo much."

I started to walk away, but I couldn't. I was convicted and had to give her forty more dollars for the second child.

Why do I tell you this story? Not to edify my giving, but to show this is exactly what the kingdom of God is all about. The emphasis is not about speaking in tongues, prophesying, and seeing how many scripture verses we can memorize. It's about loving God with all your heart, soul, and mind—and loving your neighbor as yourself. It doesn't get any deeper than that.

OUR LITTLE SUBCULTURE

The world will begin to respect us more and be more open to our message when we begin to live honestly. Mankind can see right through the phoniness of modern-day religion. They smirk behind our backs at our polyester suits. They know we think we're cool and that we are one step up the ladder from them. After all,

143

we know God, and by and large they know that we really don't like them that much.

For the most part, the Christian world has developed its own little Christian subculture, and most believers don't venture out from the safety of this cocoon often. We enroll our kids into Christian schools, we attend Christian colleges, we buy Christian CDs and Christian books, we only have Christians over for dinner, and we socialize with other Christians. Some of us work for Christian employers and some of us only hire Christians. We wear Christian clothing and Christian ball caps. We deck out our cars with Christian bumper stickers, and we only attend Christian parties and functions. No wonder we are not winning the world for Christ!

TIME FOR TRANSPARENCY

Years ago, someone told me the story of a Christian couple who invited some nonbelieving neighbors over for dinner. After the evening meal, while the adults were still at the table talking, the two teenage children in the next room got into a knockdown, drag-out fight right in earshot of the nonbelieving neighbors. The host parents called the kids into the kitchen and very calmly asked them what was going on. They each told their side of the story. The parents then asked the kids to pray and ask God to forgive them and then to pray for one another, which they did. This so touched the neighbors that they began to inquire about the church they went to. Soon they began attending, and eventually they gave their lives to the Lord.

The more the world sees us being honest, real people, the more they will see Christ. When our neighbors hear us say that we are hurting because of some misfortunate thing that has come crashing down upon our life and that we are trusting God to fix it, they will automatically focus their attention on us to see if this God we talk about so often will come through for us.

I believe that most of the nonbelieving people we are associated with, deep down in their hearts, want to believe that

God is real and that He cares about them.

It is our job to show the world that the God of the Bible is real, that He works in our lives on a weekly, if not daily basis. If we have an authentic walk with God, then we won't hesitate to let them know when we are confused, hurting, angry, or disappointed, because we know they will stand up and take notice when they see the Lord ministering to us. And if we are strong believers in God and the Bible, we know He will. It's just a matter of time.

So in a sense, we set ourselves up to be open examples of the way God moves in the lives of His children. It's a dangerous position to put ourselves in, but without doing this, they will never believe. Someone has to show the world how God works.

GOD, ARE YOU REAL?

Before I was saved, I didn't have much respect for Christians or the church. I had seen too much hypocrisy around me and had slowly but surely made up my mind that the Christians were all faking it. I wasn't even convinced there was a God, and I was raised in the church! At least if there was a God, the Christians I knew didn't know Him.

One day, when my wife had just told me that she hated me and wanted to leave, I decided it was time to find out for myself if there really was a God in heaven and if He did care about me. I found a Bible in the garage that had been packed away, and I uttered a little prayer that I don't ever want to forget. I said, "God, if You're real, I want to know because I really don't believe that You are. If You can show me that You are real, I will give You my life. But if You can't, I won't ever come to You again. Amen."

That was the only way I knew how to pray and basically still is today. I needed to know if God was genuine. No one around me showed me the reality of God. Well, He came through for me with flying colors and went out of His way to show that He was not only real, but that He had a plan for my life. I was ecstatic and remain so to this day.

NO MORE MASKS

Yes, God is real! I want the whole world to know this, but sadly enough they won't if I keep the good news to myself. I don't just *think* He's real: I *know* He is. And I know that He cares for people and will move in their lives if they only ask Him to. So I don't mind being transparent before the world because, as the Apostle Paul said, "I am well content with weaknesses, with insults, with distresses, with persecutions, with difficulties, for Christ's sake; for when I am weak, then I am strong" (2 Corinthians 12:10).

I no longer need to hide behind a mask and pretend that I don't have problems, because I serve a God who can and will show Himself to be real in those difficulties. I can't wait to show God to the world. And one of the best ways I can do this is by first sharing my problems with others, and then letting God minister to me as they watch.

It's time for us to make up our minds as to what we really believe about God. If the world sees us happy and excited about Him, they will start to get excited, too.

WHAT'S REALLY IMPORTANT?

I am thrilled every time I have the privilege of going to the pulpit to preach. I always feel that whatever God has placed on my heart is exactly what the people need to hear. One day, while I was in the middle of my sermon, I was caught up in a thought and looked down at the floor, so I could concentrate on what I was going to say next. It was then I noticed I had two completely different shoes on. I immediately spoke aloud what I was thinking: "You have two different shoes on, and they don't even match!"

Needless to say, the congregation roared as the camera zoomed in on my shoes—one dark brown and one light brown. They were similar but definitely not the same.

Some weeks later, I was making a point that was kind of

foolish in nature, so I looked down and raised up my pant legs and announced, "But at least I have matching shoes on." However, unbeknown to me, I was wearing two different colored socks!

I tell you this only to make the point that I don't go to church to make myself look good. In fact, the humor of the shoes and socks broke up any tension that might have been in the sanctuary.

My purpose in whatever I do is to cause people to see how big and good God is. Very often I tell my congregation that I'm really not concerned with what they think of me when they leave the service as much as I care what they think about God.

I've also said many times that I believe I'm the reason why some pastors go into the ministry and become failures. So often young men hang around me and see what a goof-up I am, and they see my failures and inconsistencies and think, "Hey, if God can use this guy, then He can most certainly use me."

Some of them might strike out to make ministry their vocation. What many of them forget is, you have to be called by God before you enter any kind of ministry. It's not how cool and hip the vessel is as much as it's about God's choice in calling someone into a certain type of ministry. Oh, I know we must abide by the requirements for elders and deacons given to us in Timothy and Titus, but I am just talking about plain, ol' everyday character flaws that we all have. Each of us have our own individual quirks and personality disorders.

Look at the men and women God chose in the Bible. They were far from being perfect, but God used them in spite of their imperfections.

"GOD, I QUIT!"

There was an occasion when I was about thirty-five years old when I felt unworthy to be in the ministry. And to make things even worse, there were a lot of people leaving the church during this season of my pastoring.

I had just left the home of some members whom I'd tried, to no avail, to persuade to stay in the church. (I loved these people, but their feelings had been hurt over something I'd said and done in the church, and they weren't about to be reconciled.)

As I drove down the freeway, making my way back home, I began to weep. My eyes became so blurry that I had to pull off the road for a while. I kept crying out, "God, I quit! I don't want to do this anymore. Oh, God, please let me find something else to do. I'm not worthy to be a pastor. You can find someone better qualified to do this job who can love the people better than me. Lord, I'm going to just open my Bible right now and put my finger on a verse, and if You don't speak to me supernaturally, I'm going to quit for good. Please do something big right now. Amen."

I randomly put my finger down on the page. I still couldn't see very well because of all the tears I had shed. But as my eyes regained focus, I saw the verse I had my finger on: Jeremiah 1:5. "Before I formed you in the womb I knew you, and before you were born I consecrated you; I have appointed you a prophet to the nations."

At that exact moment, I knew that it wasn't about me but about His calling. God made it crystal clear that day that I was to stay in the ministry in spite of all my character inconsistencies. Now I don't make it a practice to go around carelessly and randomly putting my finger on verses. Needless to say, that would be a very irresponsible way to live. But with that said, we must remember some of the unusual ways, according to our way of thinking, that God moved in biblical days.

I do feel that on a handful of occasions, God has instructed me to just turn my Bible open and read a verse. He always has and always will move in ways that seem foolish to both the religious Pharisees and the people in the world.

Now, there are a lot of things I can't do well, but I can love people and help them become all they can be with God in their lives. What men, women, and children desperately need is to be loved, cared for, and listened to. They don't need to be a part of a denomination, look the way we look, or even think entirely the way we think about all the various Bible doctrines. They just long to be loved, accepted, and appreciated. And I can do those things.

It's not a prerequisite to be a Bible scholar or a seminary graduate to accomplish this.

A LITTLE BOY'S PRAYER

One of my most powerful experiences of God's love came when I accepted an invitation to speak at a church just outside of Sacramento. I was at the first of the three Sunday morning services when right in the middle of worship a young boy, about ten years of age, who had what I believed to be cerebral palsy, made his way (on crutches) up to the front of the church. He came to the front row where I was standing and worshiping.

When I saw him, I bent down to see what he wanted. And he said in a rather loud voice, trying to shout over the volume of the worship team, "Mistah, are you the one who has cancer?"

I said, "Yes, I am."

He asked, "Can I 'pway' for you?"

I nodded yes, and in a very simple childlike way, he prayed, "Oh, God, 'pwease' heal this man and take all of his cancer away and make him all better. Amen."

And without another word, he turned and hobbled away on his crutches, dragging his lifeless little legs behind him as he went across the front, back down the middle aisle, and disappeared into the crowd.

It was all I could do to maintain my composure. That young boy, who obviously had plenty of struggles of his own to deal with, cared enough about me to laboriously make his way to the front of the church and pray for me. Who knows? Just maybe that is the prayer that healed me.

He never knew what an impact he had upon my life, and I will never ever forget what he did. It wasn't anything deep or profound, and it only took two to three minutes from beginning to end. But oh, what an impression he made on me.

There are people all around us who don't need much more from us than a compliment, a hug, or a prayer. Maybe the fact that we cared enough to go by the store and pick them up an extra snack for the day, or bake them a meal when they are sick is all it would take to impress them with the love of God. There are so many hurting people and so few who care.

Pray every day that God will show you one random act of kindness to do for someone else, and it will change your life in remarkable ways. It's a calling that is so simple that most of us miss or ignore the opportunity. Many Christians are so bored and uninvolved in the Kingdom life that they jump on the silliest bandwagons.

BETTER THAN A BOYCOTT

One year, around Christmas time, there was big hullabaloo about the fact that former President Bush had sent out holiday cards to people without the phrase, "Merry Christmas" imprinted on them. Instead, he had cards made with the phrase, "Happy Holidays." Many Christians heard of this and were appalled. They then took it a step further and decided to start boycotting all major department stores that were told by their employers to say "Happy Holidays" instead of "Merry Christmas."

This really touched a nerve in the Christian community. They finally had a cause, and they were ready to stand up and take the world on in Christ's name. How dare they take the Christ out of Christmas?

What didn't dawn on them was that they were several decades late in their anger and outcry. Had they not noticed that Christ had been taken out of Christmas many decades ago? I mean, if we're going to boycott stores who say "Happy Holidays" instead of "Merry Christmas," why don't we also boycott all the ones who have a Santa Claus or sell Christmas trees? Now there's a blasphemy if I ever saw one, "Trees from Christ's mass." Hello!

While we are at it, if any store sells mistletoe, Frosty the Snowman, or hedonistic Christmas lights, yuletide logs, or reindeer for the front lawn, they should be boycotted as well, because they are a direct threat to replacing the Christ-child in Christmas.

Has it ever dawned on us that the word *holiday* means "holy day?" What must the unsaved world be thinking about Christians? What about the single mom who lives down the street in a house about half the price of ours, who makes her living at the chain store that has as its policy to greet customers with "Happy Holidays" instead of "Merry Christmas?" What does she think about us and the love of God? After all, if people stop shopping at the store where she works, she could possibly be laid off and have nothing to give her kids for Christmas.

What about the clerk who I've been ministering to for the past six months? Can I no longer touch her with the love of God because I can't shop at that store anymore? Am I to tell the Holy Spirit, when I pray, that as He guides me throughout the day, He needs to keep in mind that I can't go into certain stores to minister because they are breaking all the Christmas rules? But we must have an agenda or the whole world might not think we are Christians!

Oh, if it weren't for my polyester suit, they might confuse me with some of those awful Happy Holiday folk out there. One of my concerns is that the world is really watching us more than we think, and that we are giving them an awful lot of reasons to laugh at us and not take us seriously.

It is so sad that the nonbelievers want to take the Christ out of Christmas, but what do we really expect? I guess it just means that you and I are going to have to crank up the volume a few notches and let them see the Christ of Christmas in our everyday lifestyle. I should be happy because now every time I say "Merry Christmas," they'll know—oh, will they know—that I am one of *those people,* and that's exactly what I want them to know. Maybe now they'll watch my life closer than ever, and they will see God.

THE RULE TO FOLLOW

It's all about love. It's not about boycotts, denominational doctrine, long hair, or tattoos. It's all about love.

Note what Jesus said in John 13:34-35: "A new commandment

I give to you, that you love one another, even as I have loved you, that you also love one another. By this all men will know that you are My disciples, if you have love for one another."

When Jesus keeps repeating stuff over and over, it must be very important. For example, in Matthew 5:43 Jesus tells us, "You shall love your neighbor." In Matthew 19:19, He declares, "You shall love your neighbor as yourself." He also repeats the same thing in Mark twice and Luke once. Now this is a pretty simple rule to keep.

If you were a single mom and you worked at the local chain department store, where one of the policies was that you had to say "Happy Holidays," instead of "Merry Christmas," would you want them to pray that the store from where you had been getting your only family income for ten years would close down? Probably not. You would want them to know that you had nothing to do with the stupid rule, nor did the other ninety-nine employees who worked there. You would probably still hope that other Christians would come by and encourage you throughout the day and maybe spread a little bit of Jesus' love with you instead of boycotting you.

All we have to do to make this rule work for us is to put ourselves in the shoes of other people, especially our neighbors. What would you like for someone to do for you, if you were a single mother or father and came down with a bad case of the flu? Maybe have some food dropped by for the kids, some burgers would even do, so you wouldn't have to get up and cook or go to the grocery store. After all, you have already been in bed for three days now and who knows how the kids are getting by?

I like what Jesus said in Matthew 7:12: "Therefore, however you want people to treat you, so treat them, for this is the Law and the Prophets." Not a hard rule to follow at all. God made godliness simple for us. Jesus put it this way in Matthew 10:42, "And whoever in the name of a disciple gives to one of these little ones even a cup of cold water to drink, truly I say to you, he shall not lose his reward."

THE EASY YOKE

If you were unemployed and really searching hard for a job, what might you want someone to do for you? Maybe stick a hundred dollars in the mailbox anonymously, so you wouldn't feel you owed them something back. This might be not only a nice gesture, but a godly one as well.

What could someone do for you if you were just getting over a divorce and were all alone? Would you want a person to invite you to go to the ball game with them? Or perhaps you would like a friend to make you feel like they wanted you to spend an evening with them and their family so you could enjoy some quality time together and have a home-cooked meal. It would be nice to receive a phone call every now and then just to see how you were doing.

It doesn't take a rocket scientist to figure this out, nor do you have to invest too much effort or time to do most of these things. All it takes is for us to start thinking as a *Christian.* Jesus' yoke is easy and His burden is light.

"What the world needs now is love sweet love. It's the only thing that there's just too little of." Maybe this needs to become one of the songs we sing in our church during our congregational song service. We need to let everyone know we are real people with real quirks, but we also need to let them know how to live. If you have strayed from God and want to return to Him, try going out today and find two or three people to love. Give them a verse to encourage them, or pray for them. You might even want to do some kind deed on their behalf.

Do this for two or three people and you will find God's favor coming back into your life. The kingdom has and always will be about loving others. In 1 Peter 4:8, we learn, "Love covers a multitude of sins." I like the way the Message Bible expresses it: "Most of all, love each other as if your life depended on it. Love makes up for practically anything."

Our love for others is the prescription for all sick Christians. It's the easiest way I know of to get God's attention and draw Him close to us. It doesn't take a special person to exhibit love

—anyone can do it. You don't have to be perfect to love others. God isn't looking for perfection, but He is searching for honest men and women who will reach out and touch those who are hurting.

Getting God's Attention

In the Old Testament, the main Hebrew word for "God's presence" is the *paneh*. It is used 131 times to describe the presence of God. Now, what's so interesting about this word is that it's also the same Hebrew word used 259 times for the word *face*. So, whenever we do anything in life that interests God, such as helping the poor, widows and orphans, or loving some of God's other kids, He immediately turns His face toward us to look at what we're doing. We have attracted His attention.

God can't help but be interested in situations where His will is being accomplished. Once we gain His interest by doing His will, and His face turns toward us, then instantly His presence will flood our lives.

So often when people backslide and fall away from God, they automatically think that the appropriate way to get back into His graces is to pray three hours a day and start reading countless chapters in the Bible. They try to earn brownie points with the Lord by doing extra things for Him. They direct their ministry toward God, but what they don't understand is that the best way to His heart is by reaching out to and loving His children.

God isn't asking for sacrifices; He wants our obedience. Samuel once said, "Has the Lord as much delight in burnt offerings and sacrifices as in obeying the voice of the Lord? Behold to obey is better than sacrifice" (1 Samuel 15:22).

It's all so simple that the majority of Christians miss it. The question we must ask ourselves at the beginning of every day is how many times will we serve God today? Get busy loving people. Just think what an awesome testimony we would become to the world. How many prayers of the saints would be answered if we only availed ourselves to doing God's will daily and reached out to others?

"PRAY FOR BILL"

Like Bill over here, who has just really disappointed God by committing a big sin. He doesn't think God loves him anymore, and Bills's really hurting. He cried himself to sleep the night before, and that breaks God's heart. But God doesn't have a body, so He can't go over to Bill's house, knock on his door, and encourage him. We are the only body God has on this earth. If we are daily getting into the presence of God and committing ourselves to do His will, then quite possibly while we are in our prayer closet we will hear God say to us, "Pray for Bill." And simultaneously with this impression, a verse might come or a thought to tell Bill that God loves him.

It's all so simple that often we miss it. If we sense God is saying this to us, we should write Bill's name on the tablet we carried into our closet, and beside his name we should write, "Tell Bill God really loves him and has forgiven him for all his sins."

Then, after we leave our prayer closet and head to work, we could look at the list of stuff God has laid on our hearts, get our cell phone out, and begin making some calls, beginning with Bill. If he's not home, we can leave a message on his answering machine: "Hey Bill, this is Ron. I just wanted to call to tell you that you were on my heart today, and I feel that God wants me to tell you that He really, really loves you and that all your sins are forgiven. I hope you have a wonderful day, God bless."

When Bill gets home from work still feeling despondent over his sin, and clicks on his answering machine, while he makes a sandwich, he will hear the message I've left. And immediately he will feel what seems to be a hundred-pound burden lifted off his shoulders. His joy will return and, once again, he will have hope for the future. He will be ready to get back into living for the Lord.

God's will has been done, and He is happy with us—and it

didn't take but five minutes out of our day.

How Will They Know?

As I said in the second chapter of this book, serving God is not a difficult thing. What if the whole church got jazzed up and excited about this way of living? We would probably have a revival break out over our land like we have never seen before.

I was always curious about what the Lord really meant when He said in John 13:35, "By this all men will know that you are My disciples, if you have love for one another."

How will they know? It will be through the nice things we're doing and by the concern we have for one another. The world will be so blown away they will respond: "Now those are disciples of the Lord."

Is this how it works? Well, partially. But I think there's more to it. There may be a deeper meaning. I believe that God is saying here that when we step out and start really loving one another, this will make God so happy that He will turn around and start blessing the socks off us. He will be thrilled with what we're doing, and to encourage us, He will begin pouring out His blessings. The world will see all this happening in our lives and will declare, "These are truly people of God. It's plain to see that His hand rests upon them."

Radical Servants

Paul tells us something very important in Ephesians 1:18-19 when he begins with the words, "I pray." The apostle believed that what he was about to say could only be perceived and understood if he prayed the revelation into our hearts. He goes on to explain how he has prayed that "the eyes of your heart may be enlightened (made to see and understand), so that you may know what is the hope of His calling, what are the riches of the glory of His inheritance in the saints, and what is the surpassing greatness of His power toward us who believe. These are in accordance with the working of the strength of His might."

It would do us all well to pray over these verses until we have the full impact of what He is trying to teach us. I believe the majority of believers are existing far below the standard of spiritual living that the Lord has intended. We should become better students of the Word and start committing ourselves to really understanding passages like these. The effect will significantly impact and alter our lifestyles.

However, before we can live the way I've described in this book and be a radical servant of God—daily being a spiritual sponge by going to Him and getting spiritual words and encouragement for others—we must lay all of our personal burdens, concerns, and problems on the altar. It's hard to be concerned for others the way we should be if we are always burdened with our own needs.

God has explicitly told us in His Word to cast our cares upon Him because He cares for us, and that's what we must do before we burden ourselves with the concerns of others. In fact, I believe that this is one of the main concepts behind the truth of Matthew 6:33, where Jesus instructs us, "Seek first His kingdom and His righteousness, and all these things will be added to you."

It's God's promise to us that if we truly put the needs of others before our own, then God will obligate Himself to go out of His way to meet our needs. But first we must step out in faith and put His kingdom before all else.

"FIRST-STEPPERS"

God has always called us to be what I call "first-steppers." God does very little in our lives until we step out in faith on His Word. Many don't understand this about God and His ways. For example:

- We have to step out and give our tithe to the church first, and then God will open the windows of heaven and pour out a blessing on us until we can't contain it.
- We must forgive others first, so He can extend the blessings of forgiveness to us.
- We must sow good seeds first before we can reap a harvest.
- We must confess Jesus as Lord before we can see the manifestation of salvation in our lives.
- We must pray first before God will do certain things for us.

We are the first-steppers.

It's Your Turn

After I was diagnosed with leukemia and told I only had approximately four years to live, I had a spiritual revelation while coming back from the UCLA Medical Center. I saw myself feeding the poor and taking care of the hurting and distraught, and I heard in my mind this strong voice that I perceived to be God telling me, "Go and do My will with all your heart and soul and mind, and give Me your burden of cancer. Your problem will become My problem when you radically involve yourself in My will and purposes."

Love from an honest, transparent heart will accomplish more in God's kingdom than we ever thought possible. But you might say, "I hear you, Ron, but I'm so messed up. I don't think God wants me doing His will. He has better people to choose than me."

Oh, that's just what the devil wants you to believe. You have bought into demonic thinking. It's not necessary to have things totally perfect in order to start loving others. In fact, this is the way your life will start making sense and coming together. When you become a first-stepper, God will begin to move in your life. Step out in faith and see if the Lord won't do exactly what He promises.

All of us feel unworthy to be God's stewards because basically we are. It's only an act of His great grace and love that we are the children of God. "Love makes the world go round." It keeps the planet on its axis. So start loving God by loving others today.

I think it serves us well to keep in mind the various studies that have been done that tell us that the world at large doesn't want much to do with the Church. Why? They explain that Christianity today doesn't speak to their life and that it's hard to relate to. Yet these same individuals, according to many of the surveys, admit that they really admire Jesus and like what He represents.

What does this say about the Church? Jesus didn't just sit around in His house (in fact He didn't even own one), but He went out into the marketplace and touched people where they lived. Jesus healed, taught, and loved them. Never did we see Him boycott their activities, or tell them they had to speak in tongues, or insist they had to be a part of a specific movement, or dress a certain way, nor did He condemn tattoos or the way people looked. Jesus just loved everyone and tried to help them make sense out of their lives. He had great love for the people.

Can we do less?

Eight

THE REALITY
OF THE UNSEEN

Millions of unseen creatures walk the earth
unseen, both when we wake and when we sleep.
— JOHN MILTON IN PARADISE LOST

Once you start practicing the lifestyle I've described in this book, you will automatically go deeper spiritually than you've ever dreamed possible. You will start hearing God speak to you on a continual and consistent basis. You will find the sins that so easily entangled you in the past begin to lose their grip. Plus, you will see a change in your family as they see the things God is doing in you.

The Bible tells us in 1 Corinthians 7:14 that the children of a believer are sanctified, just by the fact that Mom or Dad, or both, are in a right relationship with God. *Sanctified* means, "Set apart by God for special attention." Your family's life will be dynamically impacted by you being in a right relationship with God.

You will also find yourself filled with a sense of joy and peace that you have never before experienced. Perhaps you don't know what it's like to live without ongoing stress and discouragement. You've grown so accustomed to it that you have been deceived into thinking it's normal to feel that way. However, God never intended for His kids to live with ongoing tension, fatigue, and lack of fulfillment.

It is God's will that your needs are supernaturally met as you continue on this road of ministry and fellowship with God. I can tell you from personal experience that it is a totally awesome lifestyle. You may wonder why no one ever told you about it before—and perhaps you didn't know this way of living was attainable.

God's favor and blessings will never stop coming your way as long as you keep practicing the simple steps I've outlined in this book. Remember, Jesus said His yoke is easy, and His burden is light. Many never comprehend this because they equate simple with easy.

In Webster's Dictionary, the word *simple* is defined as, "easy to understand or deal with, not elaborate or complicated." The way to achieving God's best for your life is simple, not difficult to comprehend or achieve.

Easy, on the other hand, is defined as, "requiring no effort."

Drawing close to God through ministry and praying the way I've described is not complicated. Anyone can do it. No special training is required. Even though it is simple, some effort on your part is needed—not that much, but some.

CONSIDER THE BENEFITS

Maybe you'll need to set your alarm one hour earlier than usual. No sweat for some, but for others it might be a real sacrifice. You may have to start attending church in a more faithful manner than you are used to. You might need to lose some of the friends who are having a negative pull on your life. Perhaps your flesh might suffer some grief as you deal with a sin that once brought you pleasure. Oh, there will be a cost, but minimal when you consider the eternal rewards.

Paul wrote in Romans 8:18, "For I consider that the sufferings of the present time are not worthy to be compared with the glory that is to be revealed to us."

Most people admire an athlete who is good at what he does or a singer/musician who puts out some hot tunes. We look up to those who are exceptional at what they do and have honed their talents and rightly so. We also are very aware of the fact that people who are successful in life have put a great deal of effort into becoming the best in their field.

I am concerned that so many believe being a good Christian doesn't take any time and work, that it's supposed to come easy. But as with anything worth having, there is a certain amount of effort required if we want to be successful and mature in our walk with God. However, this is never more than we can do.

Part of the good news of the gospel is that God's Spirit will help us when we put out the slightest bit of effort.

One of the prime words that describes the Holy Spirit is the Greek word *parakletos,* which means "the Helper." When you have to deal with a reoccurring sin in your life, He will give you added strength if you ask Him. In fact, the more you become involved in ministry, the more the sin will lose its grip on you and become easier to deal with.

I didn't say it would be effortless. No one becomes a strong Christian without being diligent, but with the Holy Spirit's assistance, our part is not all that painstaking. The Holy Spirit is faithfully waiting to help all those who call upon Him.

A FALLEN ANGEL

We each have an enemy that lives in the invisible realm, and the Bible says his name is Lucifer. He used to be a high-ranking angel in God's heaven, but he severed himself from the heavenly realm because of a spirit of unbridled pride. When he was ejected from heaven and came to the earth to set up his domain, scripture says he brought along with him one-third of the angels.

In Revelation 12:4 we read, "And his (the dragon's) tail swept away a third of the stars of heaven and threw them to the earth." Now, these stars of heaven (fallen angels) help make up what we know as the demonic realm. (For further reading, see my book *Conspiracy of Silence.*)

These demons are roaming loose on the earth, and they are antagonistic toward the things of God. They particularly don't like fervent Christians accomplishing God's will. Once you become a Spirit-filled believer, they will automatically seek you out and endeavor to prevent you from fulfilling God's plan and purpose. Sadly, they have been tremendously successful in the majority of Christians' lives. Many believers have totally been defeated by these spirits of darkness and are not the least bit aware of it.

Paul tried to warn us in Ephesians 6:12 as he wrote, *"For our struggle is not against flesh and blood,* but against the rulers, against the powers, against the world forces of this darkness, against the spiritual forces of wickedness in the heavenly places."

I believe that demons and angels are a lot more involved in our lives than we choose to believe.

SATAN'S ACCESS

True, not every struggle or temptation is directly caused by demons, but probably more are than we recognize. The Bible tells us that these spirits can put carnal thoughts into our minds. For example, in Acts 5 we are told about a married couple named Ananias and Sapphira. They sold some land, and instead of donating the full price to the Church, as they said they would do, they kept some of the profits for themselves. Peter, however, confronts them: "Ananias, why has Satan filled your heart to lie to the Holy Spirit and to keep back some of the price of the land?"

The point I want you to see is that Satan had access to the minds and hearts of these two believers two thousand years ago.

In Luke 22:3, we are told that "Satan entered into Judas who was called Iscariot, belonging to the number of the twelve." In 2 Corinthians 11:3, Paul tells us, "But I am afraid that, as the serpent deceived Eve by his craftiness, your minds will be led astray from the *simplicity* and purity of devotion to Christ."

Satan keeps very active as he invades the thinking and emotions of believers. I don't understand exactly why the modern-day American Christian has such an aversion to the idea of spiritual beings. I can't fathom why we want to read books about the spiritual life if we don't believe in spirits. I have said it before, but it bears repeating: America is full of nonbelieving believers—people who say they believe in angels but rarely ask for their help.

MY GUARDIAN ANGEL

I was once traveling across the desert from Colorado to California in the early hours of the morning when I decided to start a one-way conversation with my guardian angel. It went something like this: "I know you are there, guardian angel, and I just wanted to say thanks for all the help you have given to me over the years. I know that no one talks to you, so I'm probably taking you by surprise. Don't worry about not being able to speak back to me because I know that's not easy because you live in the spirit realm. But I know you're here in the car with me."

I continued, "I wonder what you look like and what you really think about me. I'm so sorry you have to see and hear some of the stuff that goes on in my life. I hope you don't get tired of me. I know that what I am going to ask is probably really dumb. I don't even know if you have the power that some angels have to transform themselves into a human body, but if you do, I have an idea. Why don't you take on the body of a hitchhiker, and I'll pick you up?"

Then I added, "I'll know it's you, but you don't have to acknowledge being an angel because I'm sure that's probably against some rule for angels. But if you did take on the appearance of a hitchhiker, we could talk, and I could let you off and you could go back into the spirit realm. What do you say? I think it would be cool.

Well, let's see what happens."

Needless to say, this didn't happen, I wish I could tell you otherwise, but most angels have to stay in the spirit realm. Even if he were able to pull off what I'd asked him to do, I'm sure it wouldn't have been a good idea, because I probably would have gathered my friends together and tried to make that contact again and again. It could have made me lose focus—and God in His infinite wisdom knew that.

I am convinced angels are real. Many Christians say they believe in heavenly beings in the same sense they say they believe in prayer but hardly ever pray. Others say they believe in the Holy Spirit, but you never hear them say anything about Him doing anything in their lives, and rarely do they call upon Him for His help.

THE SEPARATION

Most true followers of Christ will tell you that they believe in demons, but they hardly ever do battle with them or acknowledge them in their lives. Oh yeah, there are a lot of nonbelieving believers in the world, but I certainly don't want to be one of them.

I feel that one of the main objectives of demon spirits is to get each and every child of God caught up in sin. They don't care what kind of sin or the severity of the sin; they just want a lot of sin in our lives to pre-occupy us.

Think about what Satan tried to do to Jesus in the wilderness of temptation, as recorded in Matthew 4. Three times he tried to coax Jesus to sin; knowing that if he succeeded, he could do several things in His life, one of which was to cut Him off from fellowship with the Father.

Isaiah 59:2 reveals an important point: "But your iniquities have made a separation between you and your God." *Separation* in the Hebrew means "to disjoin." In fact, it's the same Hebrew word used in Exodus 26:33 when speaking of the tabernacle. It says, "You shall hang up the veil under the clasps, and shall bring in the ark of the testimony there within the veil; and the veil shall serve for you as a partition between the holy place and the holy of holies." The Hebrew word for *partition* is the same as for *separation* in Isaiah 59:2.

This tells us that when we live in sin, our fellowship with God is cut off, and it stays separated until we confess our sin before Him. It doesn't sever our relationship, only our fellowship, which is huge. I don't even like to contemplate how many Christians are living in sin, and by so doing, they have cut off their fellowship with God and His Holy Spirit.

Being cut off from the presence of God is a dangerous position to be in. I would hate to think about living in this world without daily communion with God. Any Christian who is being led by the Holy Spirit is a dangerous force to reckon with, and Satan is well aware of this. Therefore, he will do anything in his power to block the flow of communication between us and the Holy Spirit. The devil understands that kingdom work gets done much faster when people are in tune with the Spirit.

BEWARE OF "CHANNELERS"

Most Christians don't acknowledge the demonic realm, and through their denial, they're making the demons' power so much greater. Satan and demons do not want you to be aware of their presence. They operate so much better when people don't recognize they exist. They endeavor to keep us from literally believing in their reality. Instead, they like to seek glory through making themselves out to be something they are not. For example, today many demons seek glory from people posing as spirit guides. These so-called guides have been made popular through the New Age movement. Some New-Agers consider themselves to be channelers for spirit guides—and can name the guide for whom they work.

I once read a book called *Seth Speaks,* written by a New Age channeler who had a spirit guide named Seth. The author tells how Seth discusses the affairs of the world and how we should address them.

I have also heard of a medical journal that was written by a channeler who had a very limited education. And, from what I was told, the medical journal he wrote, as his spirit guide spoke through him, was rather impressive.

These New Age channelers charge rather high prices to people who attend their seminars. If you have ever watched any of these individuals at work, it would become obvious why I associate their spirit guides with the demon spirits of darkness. Some channelers go into a semi-trance as they call for their spirit guide to come forth, manifest himself, and begin to speak. It so much imitates what I see in demonic deliverances that it's uncanny—demons boasting in their wisdom and receiving recognition and glory as they do so. It's right up their alley.

There was a New Age channeler who once visited our local community college, years ago, to conduct a seminar. So I decided to take the college group from our church to the venue site.

The channeler was supposed to present his spirit guide to the audience and receive messages, so we wanted to see just how effective he could be while we were sitting as a group just outside the building praying. We then sent a couple of kids from our group inside to see how he faired under such spiritual bombardment. We prayed with power and sang anointed songs as the channeler tried to call up his spirit guide. Thank God, he wasn't successful. His spirit guide never showed up!

MEDICATION, OR DELIVERANCE?

I believe we also see the presence of demons very plainly in some multiple personality disorders (MPDs). I have sat in college classes over the years and have listened to tormented people speak out in the voice of a second person as they converse with the first person. They will carry on a conversation within the individual in whom they dwell. And because most people with "higher intelligence" choose not to believe in God or the Bible, they label these people as having MPD. They do them a grave injustice by trying to give them counsel and medication instead of doing a spiritual deliverance on them. In many cases, this is what would set the person free.

Now, I realize that not all MPDs are of demonic origin but do have a logical medical explanation. Many MPDs truly result from a mental illness. We must be careful to not associate all MPDs with demonic possession, although I am convinced that many, if not most, are.

Demons are real and are very active all around us. The Old Testament is relatively quiet about demon spirits, although they existed in as many numbers as they did in the New Testament. They were left to do their work in general obscurity. However, we do have a glimpse of them working in a couple of Old Testament accounts.

The witch of Endor, in 1 Samuel 28:7, probably worked through the power of Satan or unclean spirits. We are also told that King Saul would have a spirit of darkness—an evil spirit—come upon him occasionally. It would cause him to grow intensely angry, and he would start hurling spears around, trying to harm people. He would become like a raging maniac whenever this spirit of evil fell upon him. David would play his harp for Saul, and the spirit would leave.

I wonder how many people in the world today, who suffer with horrible anger problems, could be linked to evil spirits. But our minds never go there because we have stopped thinking biblically.

WHOSE POWER?

In Luke 13:11, we read about a woman who for eighteen years had a sickness caused by a spirit. And we're told that she was bent, doubled-over, and could not straighten up until Jesus took authority over the problem and set her free.

Again, we don't even consider that any of our medical or emotional problems could be caused directly by evil spirits. I wonder just how many of us, who are in places of ministry, would have recommended a chiropractor or a medical doctor to the woman who had been so afflicted for eighteen years, without even thinking that her infirmity could have been more of a spiritual problem than a physical one.

Today, our worldly-minded church needs to return to a biblical mindset.

I realize that some individuals take this idea too far and see everything as being demonically linked, but I believe the majority of us don't take it far enough. Although we don't see many occurrences of demonic influences in the Old Testament, they were there. They were just operating incognito.

In hindsight, I have to wonder if spirits of lust plagued Samson or if Queen Jezebel was demonized. What about the character named Shimei in 2 Samuel 16 who, when King David came to Bahurim, ran out to where he was and started throwing stones and cursing at him. Shimei sounds a little bit touched to me, not in his right mind. I could see the Apostle Paul commanding spirits to come out of him just as he did with the woman with the spirit of divination.

We know that in Egypt, the Pharaoh's magicians were using the power of Satan to mimic the miracles Moses was performing. They made their staffs turn into serpents, something David Copperfield hasn't even been able to pull off during one of his acts. They turned water into blood and conjured up frogs to invade the land through their magical arts. They were definitely inspired by Satan and the demonic realm.

We are told that the antichrist and false prophet in the last days will operate with the power of Satan. They will raise the dead and call fire out of heaven. The enemy has power too, so don't equate everything that happens with great wonders as coming from God.

Take Authority!

Satan's power was rather subdued in the Old Testament, but when Jesus came to the earth, all hell broke loose. Jesus challenged Satan's domain. He acknowledged the spirits of darkness and openly did war with them to the point they had no choice but to reveal themselves.

Consider Matthew 10:1: "Jesus summoned His twelve disciples and gave them authority over unclean spirits, to cast them out, and to heal every kind of disease and every kind of sickness."

The Son of God knew that the apostles couldn't do the work of the ministry without having power over the world of unclean spirits. He knew they wouldn't be successful if they didn't have His power and if they failed to utilize it.

In Matthew 12:43-45, Jesus informs us about what evil spirits do when they are cast out of a body: "Now when the unclean spirit goes out of a man, it passes through waterless places seeking rest, and does not find it. Then it says, 'I will return to my house from which I came' and when it comes, it finds it unoccupied, swept, and put in order. Then it goes and takes along with it seven other spirits more wicked than itself, and they go in and live there; and the last state of that man becomes worse than the first. That is the way it will also be with this evil generation."

We are told in Mark 1:23 about a man in the synagogue who had an unclean spirit and disrupted the church service. Today, we would probably just call the police to come and arrest the guy instead of seizing the opportunity to heal him.

Scripture records how the crowds were amazed when they saw Jesus casting out spirits. They commented, "What is this? A new teaching with authority! He commands even the unclean spirits, and they obey Him" (Mark 1:27).

To challenge us even more, we need to remember the words of Jesus in John 14:12: "Truly, truly I say to you, he who believes in Me, *the works that I do, he will do also;* and greater works than these he will do; because I go to the Father."

Jesus took authority over unclean spirits and cast them out. I believe the modern church is failing miserably in this ministry. In my book *Conspiracy of Silence,* I describe a few of the deliverances I have been involved in. Believe me the demonic realm is very real.

BLINDING THE TRUTH

Demons today, especially in America, are being given free reign to do pretty much whatever they desire without any interference at all. Mark 3:11 says, "Whenever the unclean spirits saw [Jesus], they fell down before Him and shouted, 'You are the Son of God!'"

I could teach you at great length on the following passages: Mark 6:7, 7:25, 9:25, and Luke 4:33, 4:36, 6:18, 8:29, 9:42, 11:24. I could then show you how the New Testament church included demonic ministry in their era (see Acts 5:16, 8:7). The point being demons are real, and they are active in our world. The failure of the Christian church to acknowledge them is reaping for us disastrous results.

Demons aren't only in the business of making people sick (i.e., blindness, deafness, epileptic fits, and all the kinds of diseases and sicknesses that were ascribed to demons in the Bible), but they are also causing people to be emotionally unstable. Scripture tells us that they blind the eyes of our unbelieving loved ones from the truth of the Gospel (see 2 Corinthians 4:4).

Demons are using people to sow seeds of discord and disunity in the church (as Ananias and Sapphira in Acts 5). They are also involved in causing us to be so entangled in sinful desires and unfruitful activity that we are unproductive in the kingdom of God.

Sometimes our marriage problems are not as much about us (husbands and wives) as they are about destroying the life of that future little preacher boy or missionary girl who's asleep in the upstairs bedroom. Satan and his cohorts are much more aware of what's going on around us than we choose to believe.

KEEP UP YOUR GUARD

The Lord has given us authority over the realm of spiritual darkness for an important reason. God obviously knows more about the demonic realm than we do. He must have seen them as a greater threat than we do. Well-meaning Christians tell me that they don't want to give Satan too much credit. They believe that if we really love God, then demons are of little concern to us as believers.

Well, that's a nice thought, but I hate to tell you that Jesus doesn't agree with you. Jesus most likely used His authority over the demonic realm almost daily during His time on earth, and we must be prepared to do the same.

Let me make this as practical as possible. Demons are spirits, and as such, they work in the spirit realm trying to affect people with depression, discouragement, wild sinful thoughts, and temptations to do evil. They can also affect the physical body and come and go in a person's life almost daily.

When we are filled with the Holy Spirit and stand strong in the Lord, it's difficult for them to do much damage in our lives. But if and when we let our spiritual guards down (and we all do), they can quickly gain a stronghold. If we fail to use our spiritual authority and deal with them, they can reek great havoc in our life.

THWART THE ENEMY'S ATTACKS

There are practical ways you can deal with demons. First, you can use worship music to thwart off their attacks. In the Old Testament, when David played the harp and probably sang to the Lord, we are told the evil spirit would leave Saul.

Music plays a very important role in our lives. The next time you are feeling really tempted, depressed, exceptionally angry, or even sick, try grabbing some headphones and listen to some radical praise and worship music. See what the results are. You'll never know if I'm leading you in the right direction until you try it.

Speaking the Word of God is another effective weapon in our arsenal, just as it was for Jesus when Satan tempted Him in the wilderness. So, just get alone and speak out the written Word of God.

There is also the weapon of speaking to the spirits. Jesus did this, and so did the Apostle Paul. They addressed the spirits and told them to leave and be gone. Spirits are real entities, and they know that they are subservient to the demands of Christ. When they are in your vicinity and they hear YOU command them to leave, they will quickly comply. They have no other choice. Remember, the angelic realm of heaven stands behind your words of authority.

JUMPSTART YOUR SPIRITUAL WARFARE

Always keep in mind that Satan's domain wants to keep you distracted and overly busy, so you won't have time to do the things I've described for you in this book. He doesn't want you to pray and spend time with God, nor does he want you to minister to other people, including your spouse and children.

Satan doesn't care what he uses to keep you from your mission, whether it's an obsession with watching TV soap operas, a driving passion to work extra hours to make ends meet, or an out and out bondage to pornography, alcohol, or drugs. It could even be attending too many meetings during the week, including the ones at church. He desires to keep you in a confused state of mind, so you won't be able to present yourself daily to God in order to be His hands, feet, and mouth.

As you're reading, if you suddenly realize that you haven't had at least one quiet time with God this week, and you haven't been in the Word and prayer, then he (Satan) has you right where he wants you. You're already his victim. He has you under his spell.

If you come to the conclusion that it's been a long time since you called someone up and encouraged them in the Lord or helped a friend with a spiritual problem, then guess what? He has you under his spell. His plan for your life is working.

How long has it been since you prayed with your kids or spent quality time with *them—without* the cell phone or other distractions? Maybe you're being conned by the realm of darkness. It's time to wake up and jumpstart your spiritual warfare program.

An Amazing Transformation

God placed us on the earth to accomplish His will, not ours. It's time to get down to business. The Bible has called us to be spiritual people, and spiritual people live in the realm of spirits—the Holy Spirit, angels, and demons. You'll never know if what I am teaching you will work until you put it to the test. If you remain on your present course, you will probably go through the years without seeing much change. But if you begin to live the way I've described in this book, I believe the results will be nothing less than amazing. You won't even recognize your life a year from now. Spiritual growth and God's blessings will abound.

We must get back to living in much the same way as the New Testament church did. Somewhere along the line, the body of Christ is paying the price for our lack of being true and authentic.

We have seen the results of conducting church the way we've been doing it for the last several decades, and the results are not healthy. We've basically lost the majority of a whole generation of kids who were raised in church. Huge numbers of them have left the house of God and decided not to come back—perhaps for good reasons.

No More Polyester!

Let's not be afraid to reevaluate everything we've been doing. Throw out the bad and unproductive, and only hold on to that which

God tells us to hold on to. The church in America needs a total revamp—a spiritual makeover. No more polyester people!

We need to make for ourselves new wineskins, so God can pour upon us His fresh wine. Culturally, I'm not even sure that we need to go back to the New Testament way of life because God may have something else for us that supersedes that lifestyle. The early believers were right for their era, and we must be right for ours. But their dedication, spiritual commitment, belief in miracles, heart for the lost, and thirst for God's Spirit must never be lost.

I don't know exactly all God has planned for those who love Him in this century, but I do know it has to be very different than what we are used to. God wants to reach this world with the life-changing power of His gospel, but in order for this to happen, we must be willing to change the things we've been doing and the ways we've been doing them.

Why not start today?

ACKNOWLEDGMENTS

I want to give a special thanks to the following people: I want to thank my wife for staying with me and not leaving me when I was the king of jerks; my daughter Tara Crews for being the best daughter anyone could have in the entire universe—I have always been so proud of her; my son Joshua for being one of my spiritual role models and heroes of the faith; and Ashley, a daughter-in-law to die for. And my son-in-law and pastor of the Vegas campus, Jim Crews, for making me look good. And the most special thanks go to the greatest grandchildren in the whole world, Kylee, McKenzee, and Josiah Crews. They make life a whole lot better. And God! What can I say? He is everything and so much more.

FOR ADDITIONAL RESOURCES
BY THE AUTHOR, CONTACT:

RON VIETTI
VALLEY BIBLE FELLOWSHIP
2300 EAST BRUNDAGE LANE
BAKERSFIELD, CA 93307

PHONE: 661-325-2251
INTERNET: www.vbf.org